Qmail Quickstarter

Install, Set Up, and Run your own Email Server

A fast-paced and easy-to-follow, step-by-step guide that gets you up and running quickly

Kyle Wheeler

[PACKT] PUBLISHING

BIRMINGHAM - MUMBAI

Qmail Quickstarter
Install, Set Up, and Run your own Email Server

First published: June 2007

Production Reference: 1040607

Published by Packt Publishing Ltd.
32 Lincoln Road
Olton
Birmingham, B27 6PA, UK.

ISBN 978-1-847191-15-1

www.packtpub.com

Cover Image by Vinayak Chittar (vinayak.chittar@gmail.com)

Credits

Author

Kyle Wheeler

Reviewer

Russell Nelson

Development Editor

Nanda Padmanabhan

Assistant Development Editor

Rashmi Phadnis

Technical Editor

Saurabh Singh

Code Testing

Ankur Shah

Project Manager

Patricia Weir

Editorial Manager

Dipali Chittar

Project Coordinator

Abhijeet Deobhakta

Indexer

Bhushan Pangaonkar

Proofreader

Chris Smith

Production Coordinator

Manjiri Nadkarni

Cover Designer

Manjiri Nadkarni

About the Author

Kyle Wheeler is a PhD candidate at the University of Notre Dame in the Computer Science and Engineering Department. Having co-authored papers both nationally and internationally, he received an M.S.C.S.E. from Notre Dame in 2005 and expects to receive his doctorate in the field of scalable computing in 2008. As part of his PhD research, he interned at Sandia National Laboratories from 2006 through 2007.

Kyle began setting up and maintaining qmail-based email servers working for NetSeats Inc. in 2000. Since then, his client base has expanded to include the Philadelphia chapter of Notre Dame Alumni, the Church of Epiphany in the Archdiocese of Louisville, and several other groups, both large and small. He is also a frequent contributor to the qmail mailing list, which supports qmail users and administrators internationally.

I'd like to thank my family and my fiancée for their constant support while writing this book.

About the Reviewer

Russell Nelson has been a postmaster for twenty years, about half of them using qmail. In a previous life, he was Mr. Packet Driver, but people still remember him that way. Russell blogs at `http://blog.russnelson.com/`.

Table of Contents

Preface

Qmail is one of the most popular email servers. The current release was published in 1998, and has stood unchanged ever since. It has withstood the test of time surprisingly well, and a devoted community has grown around it to contribute experience, ideas, and patches to provide new features. While there is some dispute over the claim that qmail has no security flaws yet discovered, it cannot be denied that its security track record over the last ten years is unparalleled. Qmail includes several applications, including an SMTP server, a POP3 server, a QMTP server, and several related utilities for manipulating email and email storage. Qmail has been used by or is currently used by Hotmail, Yahoo!, NetZero, Speakeasy, Qwest, PayPal, Aruba.it, and others. You can learn more about qmail at `http://cr.yp.to/qmail.html` and `http://www.qmail.org/`.

This book treats qmail more as an architecture than a mail server, and from that perspective guides the reader through the installation, administration, customization, and deployment of a qmail-based server. The book begins with a quick, minimal, step-by-step walkthrough of a bare-bones qmail server, and then introduces and explains the basic design of the qmail architecture in easily understood terms.

The later chapters of the book are devoted to using qmail to provide specific features through customization and optimization. Alternative methods of providing each feature are compared, and a plethora of example scripts are provided to demonstrate the concepts and techniques.

What This Book Covers

Chapter 1 provides a quick step-by-step guide to installing a basic qmail server on a computer without an existing mail server, using ucspi-tcp and `tcpserver` to provide some of the basic services that a qmail SMTP server relies upon. At the end of the chapter is an overview of the qmail architecture that is explained in the following chapters to understand how qmail works and how the structure lends itself to customization.

Chapter 2 and *Chapter 3* mirror each other: the former details how email enters the qmail queue, and the latter details how email leaves the qmail queue. The discussion of inbound mail includes the basic architectural details as well as discussion of authentication and the two protocols that qmail supports: SMTP and QMTP. The discussion of outbound mail also includes the basic architectural details and expands into basic filtering, the definition of users and mailboxes, and remote delivery.

Chapter 4 examines in detail the storage formats that qmail supports. Specifically, it covers the factors that influence the choice of the format to be used for a given situation, using mbox, Maildir, and MH as examples. One of the most common things to do with email is to retrieve it from a central server either via the POP3 or IMAP protocols, or via a webmail interface. The latter half of this chapter covers all three, and discusses the reasons for choosing one protocol over the other, how to choose an IMAP server package, and how to set up qmail's own POP3 server.

Chapter 5 begins the more advanced section of the book with a discussion of server virtualization. Multiple kinds of virtualization are discussed, including qmail's built-in virtual domain and virtual user framework, virtual domain management software, and the possibilities provided by having multiple qmail installations.

Chapter 6 unleashes the full power of the qmail architecture's design. By altering the flow of mail through the architecture — or changing the architecture itself — qmail can be made to perform virtually any task. Sending mail without a queue, blocking viruses, detecting spam, validating recipients, and using SPF and/or DomainKeys are all used as examples in this chapter. Both lightweight and heavyweight methods of spam and virus prevention are also discussed in detail.

Chapter 7 looks at some advanced features that don't quite fit into other, larger categories, such as SSL support and optimization for mailing-list delivery.

Chapter 8 covers ongoing maintenance, monitoring, and good administrative behavior. It provides a detailed description of the log files and how to interpret them and use the qmailanalog package to get statistical analysis of qmail's behavior. Expanding the log files to contain more information, identifying and recognizing problems (including "silly-qmail" syndrome), and using information in the logs to improve qmail's performance are all explored in this chapter.

What You Need for This Book

Qmail works on practically all UNIX systems: AIX, BSD/OS, FreeBSD, HP/UX, Irix, Linux, NetBSD, OpenBSD, OSF/1, SunOS, Solaris, etc. It automatically adapts itself to new UNIX variants.

Qmail does not support Windows.

Who This Book is For

This book is targeted at System Administrators familiar with Linux/UNIX and DNS servers who need to set up qmail.

Conventions

In this book, you will find a number of styles of text that distinguish between different kinds of information. Here are some examples of these styles, and an explanation of their meaning.

There are four styles for code. Code words and files in text that are not editable are shown as follows: "Qmail's SMTP server, for example, cannot talk to the network by itself; this ability is provided by software like *inetd* or *tcpserver* or similar." Code words and files in text that are editable are shown as follows: "Qmail comes with a set of minimal install instructions, in a file named INSTALL."

A block of code will be set as follows:

```
#!/bin/sh

# Using splogger to send the log through syslog.
# Using qmail-local to deliver messages to ~/Mailbox by default.

exec env - PATH="/var/qmail/bin:$PATH" \
qmail-start ./Mailbox splogger qmail
```

Any command-line input and output is written as follows:

```
chown root ~alias/.qmail-root
chmod 644 ~alias/.qmail-root
```

New terms and **important words** are introduced in a bold-type font. Usernames have been introduced in an italicized format as follows: "However, qmail does not deliver mail to the real *root* user."

Reader Feedback

Feedback from our readers is always welcome. Let us know what you think about this book, what you liked or may have disliked. Reader feedback is important for us to develop titles that you really get the most out of.

To send us general feedback, simply drop an email to feedback@packtpub.com, making sure to mention the book title in the subject of your message.

If there is a book that you need and would like to see us publish, please send us a note in the **SUGGEST A TITLE** form on www.packtpub.com or email suggest@packtpub.com.

If there is a topic that you have expertise in and you are interested in either writing or contributing to a book, see our author guide on www.packtpub.com/authors.

Customer Support

Now that you are the proud owner of a Packt book, we have a number of things to help you to get the most from your purchase.

Downloading the Example Code for the Book

Visit http://www.packtpub.com/support, and select this book from the list of titles to download any example code or extra resources for this book. The files available for download will then be displayed.

> The downloadable files contain instructions on how to use them.

Errata

Although we have taken every care to ensure the accuracy of our contents, mistakes do happen. If you find a mistake in one of our books—maybe a mistake in text or code—we would be grateful if you would report this to us. By doing this you can save other readers from frustration, and help to improve subsequent versions of this book. If you find any errata, report them by visiting http://www.packtpub.com/support, selecting your book, clicking on the **Submit Errata** link, and entering the details of your errata. Once your errata are verified, your submission will be accepted and the errata will be added to the list of existing errata. The existing errata can be viewed by selecting your title from http://www.packtpub.com/support.

Questions

You can contact us at questions@packtpub.com if you are having a problem with some aspect of the book, and we will do our best to address it.

1
Basic Qmail

If you're diving into this section, chances are you're either entirely new to qmail, or you're looking to get a feel of this book. There are many very good qmail installation guides and tutorials that are available for free on the Internet. The current version of qmail was published on June 15th, 1998. Since then what has changed the most about the qmail experience is the accumulation of expertise and experience in using and tailoring it for the most common situations and even some uncommon ones.

Without delving into the architecture, qmail is extremely modular. In many ways, qmail is less of a mail server and more of mail server architecture. Pieces of qmail can be replaced, rearranged, filtered, and extended as necessary to achieve virtually any feature the administrator desires. However, along the same lines, qmail requires certain assistance to provide some features one ordinarily expects. Qmail's SMTP server, for example, cannot talk to the network by itself; this ability is provided by software like *inetd* or *tcpserver* or similar. This design makes qmail's components secure and much simpler and easier to verify. This design also makes the details of how the qmail components are hooked together a vital part of the system configuration, as opposed to a single monolithic server with a complex configuration file that can achieve the same thing.

To get the most out of this book, you're going to need a basic understanding of UNIX-style operating system conventions and features, simple command-line operations, and how to edit text files.

The Minimum Qmail System

Qmail comes with a set of minimal install instructions, in a file named INSTALL. It contains eighteen relatively basic steps for compiling qmail on most systems and for getting it running. These are somewhat simple, but can be trimmed even further if you're not trying to replace an existing mail server.

Compiling and Installing

Compiling qmail is generally very easy. Before compiling qmail, first obtain the prerequisites:

- A Unix-style operating system (such as Linux, BSD, Solaris, etc.)
- A working C compiler (preferably executable using `cc`, as that requires less configuration before compiling) and the standard C development system
- A case-sensitive filesystem

Having a case-sensitive filesystem is important because during installation, qmail uses several files that are different only in the capitalization of their name. For example, `INSTALL` is a text file describing basic installation procedures, while `install` is a script for putting files in the correct places with the correct permissions. The qmail distribution can be modified to work around that problem, but that is a little outside the purview of this book.

With those prerequisites, installing a bare-bones version of qmail is a straightforward five-step process as follows:

1. Prepare the system: add one directory (`/var/qmail`), seven users (*qmaild, qmaill, qmailp, qmailq, qmailr, qmails,* and *alias*), and two groups (*qmail* and *nofiles*).
2. Run `make setup install` to compile and install all the necessary binaries.
3. Run the `config` (or `config-fast`) script to create the basic configuration files.
4. Create the necessary, minimum account aliases.
5. Tell qmail where to deliver mail by default.

Simple, isn't it? Let's go into a bit more detail here.

Preparing the System

On most UNIX systems it should be relatively easy to add users and groups, using tools like *useradd, adduser, mkuser,* or something similar. For example, on many Linux distributions, the commands for preparing the system are as follows:

```
mkdir /var/qmail
groupadd nofiles
useradd -d /var/qmail/alias -s /bin/false -g nofiles alias
useradd -d /var/qmail -s /bin/false -g nofiles qmaild
useradd -d /var/qmail -s /bin/false -g nofiles qmaill
useradd -d /var/qmail -s /bin/false -g nofiles qmailp
```

```
groupadd qmail
useradd -d /var/qmail -s /bin/false -g qmail qmailq
useradd -d /var/qmail -s /bin/false -g qmail qmailr
useradd -d /var/qmail -s /bin/false -g qmail qmails
```

The users are required as part of qmail's security setup; almost every major portion of qmail runs as a different user. The reason for this is simple—it allows qmail to use standard UNIX user protections to enforce separation between its components, which communicate via tightly-controlled interfaces (namely, pipes and environment variables). This user separation is the backbone of qmail's security model—a model that has done exceedingly well and has been adopted by other security-conscious programs (e.g. OpenSSH). To complete the protection that these users provide, it's a good idea to ensure that each of these users cannot be used by anyone to log into the system. On most modern systems, this is achieved by not giving the user a working shell (e.g. */bin/false*).

Compiling and Installing the Necessary Binaries

The second step is the compilation step. Generally, this is the simplest of the steps, provided that the necessary tools (a compiler and the *make* utility) are available. Qmail will compile on most systems without further configuration, by simply executing the command *make setup check*. The exceptions are modern Linux systems that use a more recent version of glibc than version 2.3.1. On these systems, it is necessary to edit the conf-cc file that comes with qmail before compiling, so that it looks like the following:

```
gcc -include /usr/include/errno.h
```

If your compiler cannot be run using the *cc* command, edit the conf-cc file to contain the correct command to compile files.

Creating the Basic Configuration Files

The third step simply adds the most minimal configuration information that qmail requires for functioning—the **Fully Qualified Domain Name** (FQDN) of the host computer. The term "fully-qualified" means that the FQDN not only contains the host name, but also the full domain name. For example, to set up a computer named mail as part of example.com's computer network, the FQDN would be mail.example.com. To configure qmail for this computer, the minimal configuration command would then be:

```
./config-fast mail.example.com
```

The alternative command, `./config`, does the same thing that `./config-fast` does, however, it obtains the FQDN by looking up the computer's IP address in DNS. If the system is already set to go with the IP address it will always have, this is a convenient way to avoid extra typing. However, if the system's network configuration is not in its final state, using `./config` will probably produce an incorrect set of configuration files. Running either command overwrites any existing configuration files.

Creating the Necessary Minimum Account Aliases

The fourth step adds the accounts that are required by the various email standards documents (in particular, RFC 822). The following accounts are required:

```
postmaster@yourdomain.com
mailer-daemon@yourdomain.com
abuse@yourdomain.com
root@yourdomain.com
```

The last one, `root@yourdomain.com`, needn't necessarily exist. However, qmail does not deliver mail to the real *root* user, and the address is commonly assumed to refer to the administrator of the machine (for example, by scripts and monitoring programs) when the administrator needs to be notified of something. Thus, creating an alias for *root* is generally a good idea.

Aliases are defined by creating files in the home directory of the *alias* user. If the *alias* user has been created according to the above instructions, that directory is `/var/qmail/alias`. The general way of referring to this directory is `~alias/`. The alias-defining files in this directory must have very specific names, all beginning with `.qmail-` and ending with the name of the alias. For example, the *postmaster* alias is established by creating a file named `.qmail-postmaster` in the directory `~alias/`. The *mailer-daemon* alias is established by creating a file named `.qmail-mailer-daemon`, and so forth. Capitalization for account names is always converted to lowercase for delivery, so don't use capital letters in `.qmail` filenames.

The content of these files specifies exactly what should happen to email that is sent to one of these aliases. In general, the syntax is identical to the generic dot-qmail (`.qmail`) file syntax, which is discussed later in this book, but the exception is the bare minimum: an empty file. If an alias is established with an empty file, it will be delivered as specified by the default delivery mechanism (for more details refer to the *Default Mail Delivery* section).

The simplest option is to put an account name in those files, which tells qmail to forward all mail sent to these aliases to the account specified. For example, if all email addressed to `root@yourdomain.com` should be delivered to an account named *steve*, put `steve` into the `~alias/.qmail-root` file.

It is important to note that these files should have very specific permissions — they should be readable by any user, but only writable by the *root* user. This may not be the default when these files are created. To set the permissions to what they need to be, run a command that looks something like the following:

```
chown root ~alias/.qmail-root
chmod 644 ~alias/.qmail-root
```

Default Mail Delivery

The fifth and final step is to tell qmail how to deliver mail by default. *Default* means how qmail delivers all mail unless told to do something else by a .qmail file. Generally, this is done by selecting a startup script from the /var/qmail/boot directory and copying it to the file /var/qmail/rc.

In the /var/qmail/boot directory, there are several files, each of which can start up qmail with a different default delivery method. The ones that come with qmail are:

- home: Delivers email to the file Mailbox in the user's home directory.
- home+df: Supports Sendmail-style .forward files, and otherwise is the same as home.
- proc: Hands the email to procmail for delivery.
- proc+df: Supports Sendmail-style .forward files, and otherwise is the same as proc.
- binm1: Hands the email to BSD 4.4's binmail program (*mail.local*) for delivery.
- binm1+df: Supports Sendmail-style .forward files, and otherwise is the same as binm1.
- binm2: Hands the email to SVR4's binmail program (*/bin/mail -r*) for delivery.
- binm2+df: Supports Sendmail-style .forward files, and otherwise is the same as binm2.
- binm3: Hands the email to the V7 binmail program (*/bin/mail -f*) for delivery.
- binm3+df: Supports Sendmail-style .forward files, and otherwise is the same as binm3.

Unless you are migrating from an older mail server and have a reason to want the compatibility features, the file to use is either home or proc. The simplest is home.

Basic Configuration

Once all five steps are completed, a working, bare-bones installation of qmail is ready in `/var/qmail`. However, in many situations, a barebones installation is insufficient.

The basic questions to answer when configuring an email server on a new system include:

- What should be done with mail when it is received?
- Which mail should be accepted?

The most common and simplest answers to the first question generally fall into one of the following two categories: either mail should be relayed to a smarter mail server or the mail should be delivered locally.

The second question can often become far more complicated due to spam and viruses and the like, but the most basic answer is generally a list of domain names for which this email server is responsible.

As you can tell already, various answers to these questions can result in wildly different behaviors. For example, if no mail should be accepted from the network, no mail should be delivered locally, and all mail should be forwarded to a specific mail server, then this is considered **mini-qmail**. In such a situation, many of the more complex features of qmail can be eliminated. In different circumstances, the qmail server may need to accept any and all email and forward it to a central mail server (for example, a mail proxy or a caching forwarder). Or it may need to accept email for a specific domain and deliver it to system-defined users (the standard setup). Or it may need to accept email for a set of domains and deliver it locally via some virtual-domain configuration. There could be any number of additional complications, twists, and turns.

The most basic answers to these questions are specified to qmail via configuration files. Which mail should be accepted is generally specified by files in the `/var/qmail/control` directory, and what to do with mail that has been accepted is generally specified in a combination of files in the `control` directory and the `rc` file (which was set up in *Default Mail Delivery* section of the installation procedure). Note though, that the `rc` file is a shell script. Much of qmail configuration is in the form of scripts controlling how qmail and its related binaries are run.

The most basic, most important control files for qmail are: `me`, `rcpthosts`, `locals`, `smtproutes`, and `defaultdomain`. The files are not necessarily created by default or by the `./config` scripts; but they control qmail's most important functionality. They control, respectively, the name of the server, which domains' mail to accept, which domains are to be considered local once mail addressed to them is accepted for delivery, where to send outbound mail, and which domain to append to bare usernames to transform them into real email addresses. The `defaultdomain` and `me` files are simple one-line files. In the case of `me`, this line is considered the name of the server. In the case of `defaultdomain`, this line is considered the name to append (for example, `example.com`) to a bare username (for example, *user*) to construct a valid email address (for example, `user@example.com`) when necessary. The `rcpthosts` and `locals` files are simply lists of domains, one domain per line in the file. The most complex of the four, `smtproutes`, is also rather simple. Each line of the file consists of three fields separated by colons. The first field is the domain that needs to be routed this way and the second field is the domain name or IP address (in square brackets) of the server to which matching email must be sent. The third field is the port on the server to connect to, which if not present, defaults to port 25. For example:

```
somewhere.com:[1.2.3.4]
```

This line in the file informs qmail that any email sent to an address ending in `@somewhere.com` must be forwarded to the IP address `1.2.3.4`. The files `smtproutes`, `rcpthosts`, and `locals` can all use prefix-wildcards. A **prefix-wildcard** is a line that begins with a period, followed by the suffix that must match following the period. For example:

```
.somewhere.com:mail.isp.com
```

This line in the `smtproutes` file will match email addresses ending in `@here.somewhere.com`, `@there.somewhere.com`, `@anywhere.somewhere.com`, and so forth, where there is an arbitrary string and a period preceding `somewhere.com`. Note that it doesn't match the bare `@somewhere.com`. Emails addressed to matching domains are forwarded to `mail.isp.com`.

Finally there is the special case, where there is nothing to the left of the first colon as shown in the following example:

```
:mail.isp.com:1000
```

This line in the `smtproutes` file will send all email to the `mail.isp.com` server listening on port `1000`. In the `smtproutes` file, the first match is the one that is used, and this line will match anything. As such, it's usually at the end of the file.

There are many more files that qmail looks for in the `/var/qmail/control` directory. Explanations of how they work and what they do can be found in the qmail man pages, however, they are generally for more involved configuration tasks and non-basic qmail installations.

Default delivery instructions are part of simple execution.

Simple Execution

There are two primary architectural segments of qmail involved in setting up a standard SMTP email server. The first is the set of programs that work together to perform mail deliveries, either locally or remotely, and the second is the set of programs that work together to accept messages via the SMTP protocol.

qmail-start

The programs that work together to perform mail deliveries are: *qmail-send*, *qmail-lspawn*, *qmail-rspawn*, and *qmail-clean*, as well as any program that they spawn to complete their tasks (like *qmail-remote*, *qmail-local*, *procmail*, etc.). Most of these have corresponding users. In particular, *qmail-send* and *qmail-clean* operate as the *qmails* user, and *qmail-rspawn* (and *qmail-remote*) operate as *qmailr*. The *qmail-lspawn* program runs as *root*, because it must be able to deliver mail to each user as that user. In any case, all of these programs are spawned by the command *qmail-start*. This command takes two optional arguments — a default delivery command and a logging command. To understand exactly how this works, take a look at the most basic of the scripts in the /var/qmail/boot directory, home:

```
#!/bin/sh

# Using splogger to send the log through syslog.
# Using qmail-local to deliver messages to ~/Mailbox by default.

exec env - PATH="/var/qmail/bin:$PATH" \
qmail-start ./Mailbox splogger qmail
```

The first part of this script is fairly straightforward: using the *env* command to remove all environment variables before executing *qmail-start*, it then sets the PATH environment variable to make sure that the qmail bin directory is the first place searched for qmail's binaries. The second part, executing *qmail-start* with arguments, requires a little more explanation.

When qmail makes an email delivery, every delivery is made from the perspective of a program running as the receiving user, in the receiving user's home directory. Delivery instructions are treated as if they came from a dot-qmail file, with one delivery instruction per line. From that point onwards, file names are treated as mbox-formatted mailboxes, directory names (indicated by ending a file name with a forward-slash (/)) are treated as Maildir-formatted mailboxes, and commands (indicated by starting the line with a pipe symbol (|)) are all located and executed from within the addressed user's home directory. Thus, using a relative file name, such as ./Mailbox, specifies a file named Mailbox within the current directory at the time of delivery i.e. the addressed user's home directory.

In this case, the default delivery method is very simple, deliver mail to an mbox-formatted file named `Mailbox` in the user's home directory. However, the argument specifying the default delivery method can be more complex. Take, for example, the `home+df` file in `/var/qmail/boot`:

```
#!/bin/sh

# Using splogger to send the log through syslog.
# Using dot-forward to support sendmail-style ~/.forward files.
# Using qmail-local to deliver messages to ~/Mailbox by default.

exec env - PATH="/var/qmail/bin:$PATH" \
qmail-start '|dot-forward .forward
./Mailbox' splogger qmail
```

Note that because of the rules of shell-script quoting, the first argument to *qmail-start* in this case is the full text between the single quotes, or:

```
|dot-forward .forward
./Mailbox
```

Note that the single argument is, in fact, two lines. Just as if these lines were in the user's `.qmail` file, this causes the *dot-forward* command to run first, and if it returns with a code that indicates that the mail has been delivered via instructions in a `.forward` file, the delivery is considered complete. On the other hand, if it returns with a code that indicates that the user did not have a `.forward` file in his or her home directory, qmail will instead deliver mail to the `Mailbox` file, just as it would have if the `home` file's delivery instructions were used.

The text after the mail-delivery specification causes *qmail-send* to send all logging information to the program specified. In this case, the *splogger* program will be run with the argument `qmail`. The *splogger* program takes the output from *qmail-send*, prefixes it with "qmail", and logs it via the standard syslog mechanism. If neither the *splogger* command nor any other command is provided as an argument to *qmail-send*, *qmail-send* will send its logging information to standard output (or rather, file descriptor one).

To run this program by hand, simply run your chosen `rc` file, as follows:

/bin/sh /var/qmail/rc &

The ampersand at the end ensures that the program executes in the background.

qmail-smtpd

The set of programs that provide SMTP service—receiving SMTP connections (and thus, email) from the network—is organized around *qmail-smtpd*. Rather than including basic networking features in the qmail SMTP daemon executable, *qmail-smtpd*, qmail pushes that responsibility to a helper program such as *tcpserver*, *inetd*, *xinetd*, or *tcpsvd*, among others. This design decision makes for many useful opportunities. For example, the qmail SMTP service can be tested from the command-line without needing extra software by simply running /var/qmail/bin/qmail-smtpd. (Note that the DATA phase of the SMTP conversation requires CRLFs rather than simply LFs. The correct line endings can be generated by pressing *Ctrl V* and then pressing *Enter* twice.)

Getting *qmail-smtpd* to listen to the network requires extra software. Many systems come with either *inetd* or *xinetd* and they can be configured to run *qmail-smtpd* very easily. For example, an inetd.conf entry for *qmail-smtpd* might look like this (all one line):

```
smtp stream tcp nowait qmaild /var/qmail/bin/tcp-env tcp-env
/var/qmail/bin/qmail-smtpd
```

The current best practice for running *qmail-smtpd* is to use the *tcpserver* program, also written by the author of qmail, Dr. Bernstein, which is distributed as part of the ucspi-tcp package (http://cr.yp.to/ucspi-tcp.html). It can be used as follows:

```
tcpserver -u `id -u qmaild` -g `id -g qmaild` \
    0 smtp /var/qmail/bin/qmail-smtpd &
```

This command can be run manually, added to your system's startup commands, or executed using Bernstein's daemontools (http://cr.yp.to/daemontools.html) package. If added to your system's startup commands, the ampersand (&) is critical. The arguments to *tcpserver* are straightforward—first, the user and group IDs, then 0 to specify that it will listen to all network interfaces, then smtp to specify that it will use the SMTP port (25), and finally, the command to be run when a connection is made to that network port.

Standard *qmail-smtpd* does not take any run-time arguments; however, its behavior can be modified at run time by using environment variables. In particular, *qmail-smtpd* pays attention to the following environment variables:

Environment Variable	Description
TCPLOCALHOST	The DNS hostname corresponding to the local interface in the connection.
TCPLOCALIP	The local IP address in the connection.
TCPLOCALPORT	The local port number (usually 25 when used with *qmail-smtpd*).

Environment Variable	Description
TCPREMOTEHOST	The DNS hostname of the remote system.
TCPREMOTEINFO	The username responsible for the connection (usually determined using the ident protocol).
TCPREMOTEIP	The IP address of the remote system.
TCPREMOTEPORT	The port number used by the remote system.
DATABYTES	The maximum number of bytes allowed in a message.
RELAYCLIENT	The existence of this variable (even if it contains an empty string) allows the sender to relay any email message. The content of this variable is appended to each recipient address.

Most of these variables (the ones that begin with TCP) are set by the program that handles the network operations. The *tcpserver* and *tcpsvd* programs set these variables. For programs that do not set these variables (for example, *inetd* and *xinetd*), *tcp-env* will set them. The environment variable you will most commonly need to set yourself is RELAYCLIENT. If this variable is present in the environment, *qmail-smtpd* accepts any mail for delivery even if the destination addresses are not in the control/rcpthosts file. For example, an ISP that relays email from all of its customers generally adds the RELAYCLIENT variable to *qmail-smtpd*'s environment, if the connecting client is in its network.

While *tcpserver*, *tcpsvd*, and *tcp-env* will set specific environment variables, any other variable (such as RELAYCLIENT) will generally need to be set using a more generic method. Environment variables can be set in many ways, like using the standard *env* utility, the shell's *export*/*setenv* features, and *tcprules* files.

Administrative Conveniences

Qmail setup as described so far can provide full email service. This setup is, however, rather minimal, and lacks many administrative, maintenance, and troubleshooting features. Because qmail is designed to be modular, these deficiencies are easily remedied with additional programs.

About Patches

There are a great number of patches available for qmail that provide various sundry features, behavioral tweaks, and even minor bug fixes. There are two schools of thought on how to approach qmail with its plethora of patches. One is to come up with some "official" collection of patches (or just all the patches that sound sufficiently nifty or useful), apply them all, and go from there. The other is to treat qmail more like an efficient mechanism to achieve exactly what needs to be done and no more. This book falls into the latter category. There are several projects that provide "mega"-patches or that package qmail in a way that includes many patches, such as qmailrocks (`http://www.qmailrocks.com`), Bill Shupp's megapatch (`http://www.shupp.org/`), Matt Simerson's megatoaster (`http://www.tnpi.biz/internet/mail/qmail/qmail.toaster1.2.shtml`), and many others.

It is very tempting, particularly when new to qmail, to simply grab a bunch of (neat-sounding) patches and apply them all. This can be a dangerous thing to do unless you know C and SMTP well and can resolve patch conflicts. Even if the patches apply cleanly, the new features may be unnecessary and/or confusing (and may still conflict in terms of their effect). Keep in mind that qmail works just fine without them, and many of them provide features that can be obtained in other ways. Patching is an **option**, and one that should be used carefully. Every unused feature is memory (and CPU-time) wasted, and a potential source for an unexpected bug or security flaw—many patches have not been as rigorously designed or tested as qmail.

The approach encouraged in this book is one of being pragmatic and efficient (and, consequently, rather minimalist): use patches because the features they provide are necessary, and understand them before applying them. Thus, in this book patch URLs are presented alongside more lengthy explanations of the goal they accomplish and the alternatives and/or downsides.

ucspi-tcp and daemontools

The most widely recommended method for running qmail uses the daemontools and ucspi-tcp packages, both written by the author of qmail, Dr. Bernstein.

The ucspi-tcp package consists of a set of useful programs for connecting to the network and maintaining simple databases of environment-variable/connection rules. For example, *tcpserver* is included as part of ucspi-tcp.

The daemontools package contains the *svscan/supervise* programs for running, monitoring, and controlling long-running programs (daemons), and for connecting them to safe logging mechanisms (e.g. *multilog*). The default installation of daemontools creates a `/service` directory. To control a daemon with *svscan*, add a directory for that daemon to the `/service` directory. The *svscan* program starts up an instance of the *supervise* program for each subdirectory of the `/service` directory. Each of these directories must contain a shell script named `run` that contains all the necessary commands for starting the specific daemon. The `run` script must not exit until the daemon it commands exits. When the `run` script exits, the directory's *supervise* process restarts it, unless the *supervise* process has been told not to do so (for e.g. by placing a file named `down` in the subdirectory).

The combination of these two packages is a powerful setup for controlling, monitoring, and maintaining a qmail server.

Installation

Installing these packages is very simple. The ucspi-tcp package can be installed by simply downloading it (http://cr.yp.to/ucspi-tcp/ucspi-tcp-0.88.tar.gz), decompressing it, and running `make setup check` in the decompressed source directory.

The daemontools' installation is slightly more complicated.

1. You must create a `/package` directory:

    ```
    mkdir -p /package
    chmod 1755 /package
    cd /package
    ```

2. Download the daemontools source into this `/package` directory, decompress it, and move into the resulting folders, as follows:

    ```
    wget http://cr.yp.to/daemontools/daemontools-0.76.tar.gz
    tar -xzvf daemontools-0.76.tar.gz
    rm daemontools-0.76.tar.gz
    cd admin/daemontools-0.76
    ```

3. Compile and install the daemontools programs:

    ```
    ./package/install
    ```

4. If you're on a BSD system, reboot to start up the `svscan` program, or run it manually as follows:

    ```
    csh -cf '/command/svscanboot &'
    ```

    If you're using a system that uses `/etc/inittab`, you should add `svscanboot` to the `/etc/inittab`, for example, with a line similar to the following:

    ```
    SV:123456:respawn:/command/svscanboot
    ```

Using tcpserver

Basic use of the `tcpserver` program from the ucspi-tcp package has been covered previously. However, the `tcpserver` program has many options that are of importance to a well-maintained qmail installation. There are two main areas where `tcpserver` shines and is often configured according to the system-administrator's personal preference. The first is in data collection; the second is in setting appropriate environment variables and asserting behaviors based on which remote system connects to `tcpserver`.

The `tcpserver` program can collect some basic information about the remote server, as described by the possible environment variables in the previous table. However, in many cases, such information is either irrelevant or unnecessary, and the collection of such data can be eliminated to improve connection latency. For example, looking up the remote host's IP address in DNS or attempting to make an ident query to identify the remote user may not provide much benefit, but does slow down connection attempts. Turning off such queries may improve initial connection latency, if that is a concern.

For example, by default, `tcpserver` looks up the remote host's hostname in DNS. If this is unnecessary, giving `tcpserver` the `-H` flag prevents this, and consequently prevents `tcpserver` from providing the TCPREMOTEHOST environment variable to whatever program it runs (e.g. `qmail-smtpd`). Similarly, if ident information is unnecessary, giving `tcpserver` the `-R` flag will prevent it from performing that query.

The `tcpserver` program can also be configured to use a small database (in CDB format) of rules defining when to allow or deny connections and which (if any) environment variables to set, based on the data it knows about the remote host.

The most common method of specifying these connection rules is to create a text file, /etc/tcp.smtp, in a specific format that is compiled by the `tcprules` program into the CDB database used by `tcpserver` (e.g. /etc/tcp.smtp.cdb). The format of a rule in a `tcprules` file (such as /etc/tcp.smtp) is:

matcher : decision , environment-variables (if any)

Connection rules are matched on a *first-match-wins* basis. For example:

```
192.168.1.2:deny
192.168.1.:allow,RELAYCLIENT=""
=www.example.com:allow,RELAYCLIENT=""
=:allow
:deny
```

This rule file would deny all connections from the 192.168.1.2 IP address, but would allow anything else in the 192.168.1.x IP range to connect and would set the RELAYCLIENT environment variable for those connections. If the DNS hostname of the remote host is www.example.com, this file allows that host to connect and sets the RELAYCLIENT environment variable. Any other host that has a hostname (denoted by the = sign) is allowed to connect, and finally any other connection attempt (i.e. from a host without a hostname) is rejected.

This rule file can be compiled into a CDB database file as follows:

```
tcprules /etc/tcp.smtp.cdb /etc/tcp.smtp.tmp < /etc/tcp.smtp
```

The `tcpserver` program can then be told to use that CDB database by giving it the -*x* flag with the name of the CDB file, for example:

```
tcpserver -u `id -u qmaild` -g `id -g qmaild` \
    -x /etc/tcp.smtp.cdb \
    0 smtp /var/qmail/bin/qmail-smtpd
```

Using svscan

The basic format of a *supervise*-controlled service is a folder containing a shell script named `run`. This shell script eventually must run the service (daemon) that is to be controlled and must not exit until that daemon does. A good example of what might go into a `run` file is the `/var/qmail/rc` script built as part of the previously discussed basic qmail install. This script prepares qmail to run, and then runs it. As long as `qmail-start` is still running, the script does not exit. Thus, a very simple service folder for the delivery side of qmail is a folder containing that `rc` file, renamed `run`.

Logging

An extension to the previously described basic service-directory format is possible. The extension is to add a folder named `log` within the daemon's directory, which contains another shell script named `run`. In this extension, the standard output of the first first-level `run` file is piped as input to the `log` directory's `run` file. In this way, the daemon can be stopped and started independently of the logging mechanism, which can be any logging mechanism that accepts standard input, such as *splogger* or something similar. An easy, powerful method of logging is the *multilog* program (a part of the daemontools package), which saves log output in a crash-resistant, automatically rotating manner with high-precision timestamps.

Ordinarily, *qmail-start* uses the logging mechanism specified in the `rc` file, usually *splogger*. However, if the `rc` file (and thus, *qmail-start*) is controlled by *svscan*, it can be more useful to remove the logging argument from the `rc` file. This change causes *qmail-send*'s log messages to be sent to standard output, which can then be used by *svscan*'s more flexible logging architecture. There's no benefit from this if you are using the *splogger* utility, but more powerful logging tools, such as *multilog*, do benefit from the change. The `run` file for the *qmail-send* service directory might look something like the following:

```
#!/bin/sh
exec env - PATH="/var/qmail/bin:$PATH" \
qmail-start ./Mailbox
```

A log/run file for the *qmail-send* service directory might look similar to the following:

```
#!/bin/sh
exec setuidgid qmaill multilog t /var/log/qmail/qmail-send/
```

The beginning of this command, *setuidgid qmaill* uses the *setuidgid* tool from the ucspi-tcp package. The previous command is essentially equivalent to the following:

```
exec su qmaill -c 'multilog t /var/log/qmail/qmail-send/'
```

This is because both switch to a different user (*qmaill*) before running the rest of the command, but the *setuidgid* version is easier to read and type. The reason for using the *qmaill* user for logging is that it prevents the logs from being altered even if an attacker controls the process generating the logs (*qmail-send*, in this case).

This same structure can be used for running *qmail-smtpd* in a controllable, monitorable fashion. Simply create a directory for it (e.g. /var/qmail/supervise/smtpd) and create a run file for it, such as:

```
#!/bin/sh
QUID=`id -u qmaild`
QGID=`id -g qmaild`
LOCAL=`head -1 /var/qmail/control/me`
if [ ! -f /var/qmail/control/rcpthosts ]; then
    echo "Without a rcpthosts file, qmail is an open relay."
    echo "Open relays are spammer havens."
    echo "Please use a rcpthosts file."
    exit 1
fi
exec tcpserver -R -l "$LOCAL" -H \
    -x /etc/tcp.smtp.cdb \
    -u "$QUID" -g "$QGID" \
    0 smtp \
    /var/qmail/bin/qmail-smtpd 2>&1
```

Then create in that directory another directory named log, and in the log directory, a run file such as:

```
#!/bin/sh
exec setuidgid qmail multilog t /var/log/qmail/smtpd/
```

Once these files are created, telling *svscan* to use them to control the service they specify is a two-step process. First, make sure that the run files are executable:

```
chmod +x /var/qmail/supervise/smtpd/run

chmod +x /var/qmail/supervise/smtpd/log/run
```

Then link the daemon's directory into `/service`, as follows:

```
ln -s /var/qmail/supervise/smtpd /service/qmail-smtpd
```

Wait a few moments, and then run the following to double-check that all is well.

```
svstat /service/qmail-smtpd
```

If it started as it should, the output of that command should indicate that the service in question (*qmail-smtpd*) has been running for a few seconds already. You can perform essentially the same procedure on the *qmail-start* service directory, or any other daemon to be controlled by *svscan*.

Once *svscan* is controlling a folder and the associated daemon, you can command the daemon with the *svc* command. For example:

```
svc -d /service/qmail-smtpd
```

This will order the *qmail-smtpd* service to stop by sending it a TERM signal. Using the *-h* flag instead of *-d* will cause the service to receive a HUP signal; in the case of *qmail-start*, this causes qmail to re-read many of its configuration files. This reread-config-on-HUP is a behavior shared by many UNIX daemons. The *-u* flag will cause the service to start again after having been stopped by the *-d* flag. The *-t* flag, like the *-d* flag, also sends a TERM signal. However, unlike the *-d* flag, the service is restarted as soon as it exits.

It is important to note that the TERM signal sent by the *-t* and *-d* flags does not cause all daemons to exit immediately. For example, when *qmail-send* receives a TERM signal, it finishes all deliveries currently in progress before exiting — which means that it may take several minutes to exit. To bring a daemon down immediately, use the *-k* flag, which sends the un-ignorable KILL signal. Note, though, that while the KILL signal will immediately terminate any process not protected by the kernel, the signal is not propagated to any of the daemon's child processes. Also, the *-k* flag alone allows the server to restart once it exits (similar to the *-t* flag). Thus, it is often used after the *-d* flag has been used first, to terminate a recalcitrant daemon.

The Overall Structure of Qmail

Before delving too deeply into further configuration and tailoring of qmail, it is important to understand the basic structure of qmail. Qmail is often referred to as merely a mail server software package. While this may be accurate in one sense, it is more accurate to think of qmail as a mail delivery architecture whose architect has thoughtfully provided a basic implementation of all the components of that architecture.

Qmail is very modular—it consists of a series of simple programs communicating via specific and limited interfaces. Each simple program has a specific and limited task to perform. This architecture allows each component program to be easily replaced or new programs to be inserted between the basic components.

Additionally, this architecture limits the security impact of any one of the components. Each program is further separated from the others, whenever possible, by giving each program a different UNIX user and specific permissions so that it can't affect anything it is not supposed to. Because the communication interfaces are limited, it is significantly more difficult to attack the software and achieve much—attacking a component that does not have enough privileges to do anything other than what it is supposed to do is much less useful for an attacker.

The simplest example is receiving email from the network. The trail of programs in basic qmail is as follows: `tcpserver` to `qmail-smtpd` to `qmail-queue`. The `tcpserver` program has two tasks: open up a port to listen to the network, and run `qmail-smtpd` as the appropriate user for every connection. Because listening to low ports (such as the SMTP port, 25) requires *root* permissions, `tcpserver` generally runs as *root*. However, because `tcpserver` doesn't attempt to understand the communication, it is very difficult to attack. The `qmail-smtpd` program has only two tasks as well: speaking the SMTP protocol sufficiently to receive email messages, and sending these email messages to `qmail-queue`. As such, `qmail-smtpd` need not do anything with the on-disk queue or the network. This allows `qmail-smtpd` to be run as a user with very limited permissions, and also allows `qmail-smtpd` to be a much simpler, and easier to verify and debug, program than it would be otherwise, even though it has to interact directly with user (or attacker) input. The `qmail-queue` program has only one task—to write messages to the on-disk queue prepended with a Received header. It need not talk to the network, or understand the contents of the messages it writes to disk, making the program simple and easy to verify and thus hard for an attacker to break.

Note that this architecture can be easily extended. The `tcpserver` program can execute any program, which can in turn execute `qmail-smtpd` as necessary. This might be useful, for example, to make decisions about whether to permit a connection to reach `qmail-smtpd` or to set and unset environment variables before `qmail-smtpd` is executed. It could even be used to sanitize data before it gets to `qmail-smtpd`. Similarly, while `qmail-smtpd` normally executes `qmail-queue`, it may invoke any program. This program can then execute `qmail-queue` as necessary, which might be useful, for example, to filter out email messages that contain viruses.

As another example, the *qmail-start* program executes several programs: *qmail-send*, *qmail-lspawn*, *qmail-rspawn*, and *qmail-clean*. Each of these programs has a specific task. *qmail-send* must monitor the on-disk queue of mail and route mail appropriately by commanding either *qmail-lspawn* or *qmail-rspawn* to deliver the message depending on whether the message should be delivered to a local user or a remote user, respectively. Once messages have been delivered, it commands *qmail-clean* to remove the message from the queue. Both *qmail-lspawn* and *qmail-rspawn* receive delivery commands and spawn the necessary number of instances of *qmail-local* and *qmail-remote* to do the actual delivery. The *qmail-remote* program is a simple program that reads an email from standard input, and delivers it to the hosts and recipients specified to it by arguments. It does not have sufficient permissions to read out of the queue itself, and so must be handed the message to deliver. It can even be used alone as follows:

```
echo message | qmail-remote \
    smtp.example.com sender@example.com recipient@example.com
```

The *qmail-local* program is also simple; its task is to read an email from standard input and deliver it to the specified local user, using the procedures detailed in that user's .qmail files. Like *qmail-remote*, it does not have sufficient permissions to read or modify the on-disk queue.

Each of these programs is independent of the others, and relies only on the interface provided to it. By restricting the permissions that each component has, both attacking the system as well as achieving much with a single compromised component is made significantly more difficult. This is the fundamental concept behind the privilege-separation security technique employed by qmail.

The following diagram depicts this description graphically:

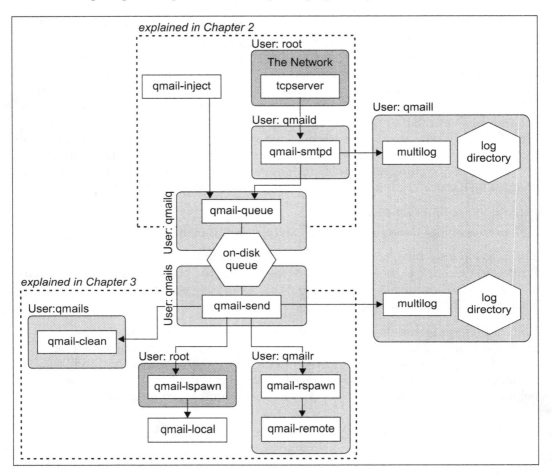

In this diagram, each on-disk element is a hexagon, each process is a rectangle, and each separate user-protected domain is a tinted rounded-rectangle (*root* domains are darker). The arrows indicate the direction email travels through the system. As you can see, the central feature of the qmail architecture is the on-disk queue. Despite its centrality, very few components of qmail need to read or modify the queue.

Summary

This chapter has laid out the most fundamental details of qmail: first how to install a minimal qmail server, then convenient means of controlling the qmail server, and finally the basics of the qmail architecture. The fundamental innovation of qmail is its architecture, and as such the rest of this book is devoted, in one way or another, to examining and exploiting the benefits of that architecture. The next chapter talks about the input end of the qmail mail system.

The next two chapters talk about how to operate the queue—first putting messages into the queue and then controlling how messages exit the queue. In essence, the next two chapters focus on the top and bottom halves, respectively, of the qmail architecture.

2

Getting Email into the Queue

This chapter covers the input end of the qmail mail system. It focuses on the SMTP protocol and related protocols, and the details of how the *tcpserver*, *qmail-smtpd*, and *qmail-queue* programs provide that service.

qmail-queue and the Qmail Queue

The following diagram is a part of the overall structure of qmail described in Chapter 1.

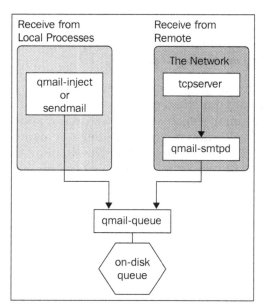

The only way of getting email into the on-disk queue in qmail is to use the *qmail-queue* program. This is a simple program with a single task: take an email and store it in the on-disk queue.

Any program can use `qmail-queue` to inject a message into the queue, provided it can present the email message and the envelope information (the sender and the list of recipients) in the form that `qmail-queue` requires.

The on-disk queue is somewhat complicated. It is the communication and storage mechanism used for handing messages to the `qmail-send` component. The `qmail-queue` program handles the details of injecting messages into the queue, just as the `qmail-clean` program handles the details of removing messages from the queue. It is often tempting to attempt to manipulate the queue directly — for example, to remove a message from it. Naïvely modifying the queue, however, is a quick way to corrupt the queue and make `qmail-send` behave in unpredictable ways. The correct way to modify the queue is to stop `qmail-send` and use a queue modification tool (such as `qmHandle`, `qmqtool`, or `qqtool`).

Each message in the queue is represented by several files. Which files compose a message depends on the current delivery state of the message.

Viewing the current state of the queue, however, is very simple. The program `qmail-qstat` displays the number of messages currently in the queue and how many are currently being injected into the queue. The `qmail-qread` program lists each message in the queue with the date and time the message was injected into the queue, the message's sender, and the list of recipients. With each recipient, `qmail-qread` provides an indication of whether the message has been delivered to that recipient and, if not, whether the recipient is considered a *local* recipient (whose delivery will be handled by qmail) or a *remote* recipient (whose delivery requires the message to be relayed to another mail server).

There are two primary methods qmail provides for supplying `qmail-queue` with messages: the local execution method and the remote method. Programs running on the same machine as qmail — such as `cron`, `atd`, `mail`, and any user's email program — use the local execution method for sending email. Local execution means that these programs feed the message to either the `sendmail`, `qmail-inject`, or `qmail-queue` program. The remote method accepts incoming email messages via the network (usually using the SMTP protocol).

The qmail-inject and sendmail Interfaces

The `sendmail` program and the `qmail-inject` program are convenient ways of sending mail from a program running on the same computer as the qmail server.

Of the two, `qmail-inject` is the more basic one. Its simplest invocation, sending an email that is stored in a file named `message`, can be done as follows:

```
qmail-inject <message
```

Part of the simplicity of this is that `qmail-inject` expects the input file to be a correctly formatted email message, complete with correctly formatted headers. The headers may be used as a last resort to guess the envelope recipients (`qmail-inject` searches for To:, Cc:, Bcc:, Apparently-To:, Resent-To:, Resent-Cc:, and Resent-Bcc: headers, in that order) and the envelope sender (`qmail-inject` searches for Sender:, From:, Reply-To:, Return-Path:, Return-Receipt-To:, Errors-To:, Resent-Sender:, Resent-From:, and Resent-Reply-To: headers, in that order). However, it is better to specify the envelope information with the command-line either as arguments to `qmail-inject` or by defining specific environment variables. While `qmail-inject` has a low tolerance for incorrectly formatted headers, if important headers are missing (for example, From:), `qmail-inject` will insert them using information it has gained through other methods (i.e. arguments or environment variables). A simple correctly formed message looks like this:

```
From: me@here.com
To: someone@somewhere.com
Subject: An Example Message

This is the body of the example message.
```

As an example of defining the envelope senders and recipients on the command line, if a message to be sent is stored in a file named `message`, and the message must be sent to the email address `someone@somewhere.com` from the email address `me@here.com`, then sending the message works as follows:

```
qmail-inject -fme@here.com someone@somewhere.com <message
```

The `qmail-inject` program is, of course, qmail-specific. Many programs (such as `mail`, `crond`, and PHP, among others) expect a program named `sendmail` to be available for sending email. This convention originated from the fact that the Sendmail email server was the universal standard. Besides, it is also very useful to have a standard interface for sending an email that is independent of the specific email server. Thus, qmail also provides a `sendmail` executable, which emulates the basic email sending behaviors of the Sendmail `sendmail` program. Making this program available in */usr/bin/sendmail* is all that is needed to allow most common email programs to send email. Qmail's `sendmail` program uses `qmail-inject` to do the actual work and merely translates Sendmail-style arguments into the necessary forms for `qmail-inject`.

The `qmail-inject` program expects, as input, a message with correctly formatted email headers. It does not do any further validation or correction of email content, and so can permit badly formed messages to be queued. Badly formatted headers, however, can confuse it and cause it to refuse to send the message to `qmail-queue`. Because the `sendmail` program uses `qmail-inject`, it is subject to the same restrictions. In cases where it may be difficult to ensure that headers are correctly formatted, the *new-inject* program, from the mess822 package (http://cr.yp.to/mess822.html) can correct many badly formed message headers. The *new-inject* command can be used as a drop-in replacement for *qmail-inject*.

qmail-smtpd and the QMAILQUEUE Patch

Receiving email from the network via the SMTP protocol is perhaps the most common use of qmail. As described before, *qmail-smtpd* is run by another program that handles all the networking details. The behavior of *qmail-smtpd* is affected by environment variables. For the purpose of this book, discussion is limited to using *tcpserver* with *qmail-smtpd*, but the basic techniques discussed here apply to whatever software is used in its stead.

Accepting or Rejecting Email

When a remote machine connects and talks to *qmail-smtpd*, *qmail-smtpd* has two primary responsibilities: determining whether the message should be accepted, and if it should, then handing the message to *qmail-queue* for injection into the on-disk queue. *qmail-smtpd* uses four key pieces of information to decide whether to accept each message and hand it to *qmail-queue*:

1. The recipients of the message
2. The existence of the RELAYCLIENT environment variable
3. The size of the message
4. The message's envelope sender

The first two in the list are positive reasons: they cause the message to be accepted. The last two are negative reasons: they cause the message to be rejected. Submitted email messages are not accepted unless one of the first two reasons applies. However, the last two tests are also applied and can overrule the first two.

The size of the message is probably the most obvious reason to reject a message. If the message cannot be stored on the disk, it simply cannot be accepted for delivery. The *qmail-smtpd* program doesn't necessarily know whether the queue currently has enough space for the message because *qmail-smtpd* doesn't touch the queue. That is *qmail-queue*'s prerogative. However, *qmail-smtpd* doesn't always have to invoke *qmail-queue* to make a decision about the message's size; a size limit may be specified (in bytes) in the control/databytes file or in the DATABYTES environment variable. Any message exceeding the limit is not accepted, and if no limit is specified, *qmail-smtpd* will not reject a message based on its size.

The address of the sender is perhaps an unlikely reason for `qmail-smtpd` to accept or reject a message. However, qmail contains a simple (albeit ineffective against modern spammers) anti-spam mechanism that instructs `qmail-smtpd` to reject messages based on the sender. The file `control/badmailfrom` is interpreted as a list (one per line) of email addresses that, if used as the envelope sender of a message sent to `qmail-smtpd`, cause the message to be rejected. Each line may also contain lines with only an at sign (@) and a domain name, which instructs `qmail-smtpd` to reject messages from any address ending with that domain name.

The recipients of a message—or more precisely, the envelope recipients—are an understandable detail that `qmail-smtpd` uses to decide whether to accept a message. For example, if the qmail server is set up to receive email for `example.com` (in other words, `example.com` is listed in `control/rcpthosts`), and if the recipient of an incoming message is `somebody@example.com` the message is accepted and given to `qmail-queue`.

The most flexible of the four pieces of information `qmail-smtpd` uses to decide whether to accept an email is the existence of the `RELAYCLIENT` environment variable; flexible because wrapper applications can use this for any purpose.

RELAYCLIENT and Authentication

The basic semantics of the `RELAYCLIENT` variable are that if it exists, the message is accepted; otherwise the message is accepted only if one of the recipients' domains is in the `control/rcpthosts` file. This variable can be set for any reason. For example, the `tcpserver` program allows environment variables to be set based on the IP address or DNS hostname of the remote machine sending the message.

tcprules

As a basic example, ISPs frequently have the policy that any of their customers may send email through the ISP's mail server. To implement this, they tell `tcpserver` to set the `RELAYCLIENT` variable for all clients whose IP address is in the ISP's pool of client addresses.

The `tcpserver` program can use CDB databases created by the `tcprules` program to make decisions about whether to allow or reject a connection and, if it is allowed, what environment variables to set. To implement the previously described ISP's policy, assuming all the clients have addresses in the B-class network `192.168.x.x`, the necessary `tcprules` file would look like the following (because only the first matching rule is used):

```
192.168.:allow,RELAYCLIENT=
:allow
```

However, if they want to refuse messages from anyone other than their clients, then they would use the following:

```
192.168.:allow,RELAYCLIENT=
:deny
```

Further details of the syntax of the `tcprules` file and the use of the `tcprules` program are in the `tcprules` manual (`http://cr.yp.to/ucspi-tcp/tcprules.html`).

The `RELAYCLIENT` environment variable can be used for more than simply making `qmail-smtpd` accept email. The behavior described so far is obtained by simply creating the variable versus not creating it. If the variable is not empty, the contents of the variable are appended to each recipient email address as the message is accepted. For example, if `RELAYCLIENT` contains the string "FOO", a recipient `someone@here.com` is altered to `someone@here.comFOO`. This is primarily useful for changing the delivery actions based on where the message came from, or to redirect email entirely, such as if `RELAYCLIENT` contained the string "-forwarded@elsewhere.com". The appended string becomes a part of the recipient's address before the message is evaluated by `qmail-send`, and may completely alter the destination. The previous example's recipient would, in this situation, become `someone@here.com-forwarded@elsewhere.com`.

The `RELAYCLIENT` variable may also be used for authenticating senders who are allowed to send mail but who do not always have a predictable IP address. This is achieved in many ways; the most common ways are POP-before-SMTP (or IMAP-before-SMTP) and SMTP-AUTH (or SMTP authentication).

POP-before-SMTP

Originally, the SMTP protocol was not written with an inherent method of authenticating a user, such as the standard username-and-password formula that is so prevalent. One way of addressing this drawback is to connect SMTP with another protocol that *does* support some form of authentication. One common protocol used for this purpose is the POP3 protocol, though technically any protocol that supports authentication of some kind (such as IMAP or HTTP) can be used. The basic idea is that when a user authenticates with this other protocol, the server will record the IP address of that user. This record then causes the SMTP server to consider all communication with that IP address authenticated for a limited time.

This is made relatively easy by the checkpassword-compatible authentication tools—commonly used with `qmail-pop3d`—which run a specified program upon successful authentication.

For example, the standard way to run *qmail-pop3d* (ignoring *tcpserver* for the moment) is as follows:

```
qmail-popup mail.example.com \
    checkpassword \
    qmail-pop3d ./Maildir/
```

This requires a little explanation. The *qmail-popup* program requests the username and password from the user, which it validates using the program mentioned after the domain name in its arguments — in this case, the *checkpassword* program. If the username and password are correct, the *checkpassword* program changes to that user's home directory and runs the program specified in the remaining part of its argument list — in this case, the *qmail-pop3d* program. The *qmail-pop3d* program then provides the POP3 protocol for reading the contents of the specified mailbox — in this case, ./Maildir/.

Assuming the usual environment variables have been set, one can easily add a script in between *checkpassword* and *qmail-pop3d* to perform the necessary bookkeeping to save the IP address of the just-authenticated computer. For example, a script named saveip.sh:

```
#!/bin/sh
touch /authenticated/$TCPREMOTEIP
exec "$@"
```

This script can be added to the previous execution line as follows:

```
qmail-popup mail.example.com \
    checkpassword \
    saveip.sh \
    qmail-pop3d ./Maildir/
```

If authentication is successful, *checkpassword* will run the saveip.sh script. This script creates a file in the /authenticated directory whose name is the IP address of the client that just authenticated itself and then runs the program specified in its arguments. Checking the /authenticated directory for files created in the last ten minutes is done with another script (such as checkauth.sh):

```
#!/bin/sh
TIMESTAMP=/tmp/$$.stamp
touch -d "10 minutes ago" $TIMESTAMP
test -f /authenticated/$TCPREMOTEIP -a \
    $TIMESTAMP -ot /authenticated/$TCPREMOTEIP && \
    export RELAYCLIENT="" || \
    rm -f /authenticated/$TCPREMOTEIP
rm -f $TIMESTAMP
exec "$@"
```

Now, as an alteration to the *qmail-smtpd* execution line from Chapter 1:

```
exec tcpserver -R -l "$LOCAL" -H \
    -x /etc/tcp.smtp.cdb \
    -u "$QUID" -g "$QGID" \
    0 smtp \
    checkauth.sh \
    /var/qmail/bin/qmail-smtpd 2>&1
```

This makes *tcpserver* run the checkauth.sh script instead of *qmail-smtpd*. This script runs *qmail-smtpd* itself once it has performed its magic and potentially creates the RELAYCLIENT environment variable. Thus, when *qmail-smtpd* runs, if the same client has authenticated via POP3 in the last ten minutes, the RELAYCLIENT environment variable is set, and *qmail-smtpd* allows that client to relay email.

SMTP-AUTH

Using POP-before-SMTP can be rather inconvenient. It requires that the users check their email via the POP3 protocol before being allowed to send via the SMTP protocol. Since POP3 and SMTP are not inherently connected, email clients rarely make connecting them this way very convenient. Also, when using a non-qmail POP3 server, or running the POP3 server on a separate machine from the SMTP server, saving the authenticated IP address can be difficult (though not impossible) to implement.

Fortunately, most email clients these days support an extension to SMTP called SMTP-AUTH that adds support for authentication to the SMTP protocol. Unfortunately, basic *qmail-smtpd* does not support SMTP-AUTH. There are two primary ways of adding this feature.

The first method is to provide a replacement to *qmail-smtpd* that understands SMTP-AUTH. The classic example of this sort of software is Bruce Guenter's *mailfront* program (http://untroubled.org/mailfront/), which also provides several other useful features. Another good example is Linux Magic's *magic-smtpd* (http://www.linuxmagic.com/opensource/magicmail/magic-smtpd/), which provides even more features.

The second method is to patch *qmail-smtpd* so it supports SMTP-AUTH itself. There are several such patches available, some of which have conflicting semantics, so be careful that the documentation matches the patch exactly. One of the best maintained patches is maintained by Dr. Erwin Hoffman (http://www.fehcom.de/qmail/smtpauth.html). The main drawback of this method is that it conflicts with some connection-encryption technologies, particularly the SSL patch to *qmail-smtpd*.

Which of these methods is best to use depends on your particular needs. The security consequences of both options are essentially the same. Using replacement software (i.e. *mailfront* or *magic-smtpd*) is particularly good for people who wish to avoid using source patches and dealing with potential patching errors. On the other hand, there is a larger existing library of potential features that can be added to *qmail-smtpd* via a patch than to these replacement packages. Additionally, patching *qmail-smtpd* allows the administrator to limit the code that is included in their SMTP daemon. Packages like *mailfront* provide additional features, but not all of them are useful in all cases, and unused features represent (at some level) wasted memory. In essence, using a replacement is simpler, but patching *qmail-smtpd* is more flexible and potentially more resource efficient.

The QMAILQUEUE Patch

In some cases, it is desirable to filter messages in a slightly more complex or extensible way than has been described so far. For example, one may want to scan all incoming messages for viruses, or for spam, or for some other purpose. The message may need to be either modified or blocked based on this filter.

An extension to *qmail-smtpd* that allows for such filters is known as the QMAILQUEUE patch (http://www.qmail.org/qmailqueue-patch). The basic idea of this patch is that *qmail-smtpd* hands email to the program specified in the QMAILQUEUE environment variable rather than the standard *qmail-queue* program.

This patch is used to accomplish many things. For example, the QMAILQUEUE environment variable can point to Inter7's *simscan* program (http://www.inter7.com/?page=simscan). The *simscan* program writes each message to a temporary location where it then runs a virus scanner (such as ClamAV, available at http://www.clamav.org) and/or a spam scanner (such as SpamAssassin available at http://spamassassin.apache.org) on it. *simscan* then takes action based on the results of these programs. For example, if the message contains a virus, or has a spam score that is too high, *simscan* can exit with an error code rather than handing it to *qmail-queue*, thus causing *qmail-smtpd* to reject the message.

The program specified in the QMAILQUEUE environment variable is not required to relay the message to the real *qmail-queue* program unchanged. The *qmail-dk* program (available at http://qmail.org/) adds a DomainKeys signature or validation result header to messages before delivering them to *qmail-queue*. This technique can chain together multiple programs to create much more complicated filters. For example, *qmail-dk* can be configured to hand messages to *simscan*, which then sends the messages to *qmail-queue*.

Note, however, that once `qmail-smtpd` hands the message to the next program in the chain, its only responsibility is to report any errors from that program to the connected client. It does not retain control of the email, but instead trusts that the `qmail-queue`-compatible program (or wrapper) it has called will either queue the message successfully or return a failure code.

Other Mail Protocols

`qmail-smtpd` is the most common method of accepting email messages for delivery from the network, but it is not the only one that comes with qmail. There is another program that comes with qmail called `qmail-qmtpd`. As the name indicates, just as `qmail-smtpd` is a **Simple Mail Transfer Protocol (SMTP)** server, the `qmail-qmtpd` program is a **Quick Mail Transfer Protocol (QMTP)** server.

While SMTP is the standard protocol for email transmission on the Internet, there are many email servers and clients that do not strictly adhere to the definition and requirements of SMTP. Most of them, however, deviate from the SMTP standard in predictable, common ways. This has become, in essence, a distinct de-facto protocol that was dubbed by Dr. Bernstein the **Old-Fashioned Mail Injection Protocol (OFMIP)**.

Quick Mail Transfer Protocol (QMTP)

QMTP is a protocol invented by the author of qmail, Dr. Bernstein, to address some of the inefficiencies in the SMTP protocol. For example, the commands are not blocking (which is only partially addressed by the SMTP PIPELINING extension) and use fewer bytes to transmit the same information. QMTP has not garnered widespread popularity for delivering mail across the Internet; however, it can be useful for transferring messages between servers in the same organization. Besides `qmail-qmtpd`, another tool in the qmail package that speaks QMTP is `maildir2qmtp`, which takes a given Maildir-formatted mailbox and transmits all the messages in it to a specified computer using QMTP.

To be able to receive email via QMTP as well as SMTP, simply start up another instance of `tcpserver` on port 209, in a similar fashion to the SMTP server. An example `run` file, based on the `qmail-smtpd` run file, looks like the following:

```
#!/bin/sh
QUID=`id -u qmaild`
QGID=`id -g qmaild`
LOCAL=`head -1 /var/qmail/control/me`

if [ ! -f /var/qmail/control/rcpthosts ]; then
    echo "Without a rcpthosts file, qmail is an open relay."
```

```
        echo "Open relays are spammer havens."
        echo "Please use a rcpthosts file."
        exit 1
fi

exec tcpserver -R -l "$LOCAL" -H \
    -x /etc/tcp.smtp.cdb \
    -u "$QUID" -g "$QGID" \
    0 209 \
    /var/qmail/bin/qmail-qmtpd 2>&1
```

It is important to point out that *qmail-send* does not use QMTP. It is possible to add this support to qmail via a patch by Russ Nelson (http://www.qmail.org/ qmail-1.03-qmtpc.patch). The patch alters *qmail-remote* to understand the QMTP extension to standard MX priorities. Normally, *qmail-remote* looks up the MX records of the destination address (or A records if no MX records exist) in DNS, examines the MX priority information, and attempts to send the mail to the listed MX servers in order of priority. With the patch, if there is an MX record with a priority between 12800 and 13055 (normally, SMTP hosts don't use a priority greater than about 1000), it identifies the site as one that receives mail via QMTP in addition to SMTP. Thus, *qmail-remote* uses QMTP to transfer the mail rather than SMTP. By the same logic, to advertise that a system is capable of receiving mail via QMTP, it needs an MX record with a priority between 12800 and 13055.

Old-Fashioned Mail Injection Protocol (OFMIP)

There are no standard documents defining the deviations from the defined SMTP standard that make up the de-facto OFMI protocol. However, the general behavior is that an OFMIP server performs many transformations on the messages that it receives—usually to make accepted messages conform to the SMTP specification.

For example, while an SMTP server is directed to deliver messages only to recipient addresses in the form user@fully-qualified-domain-name, an OFMIP server accepts addresses that are simply user or user@host and will transform the address into the SMTP-required fully qualified form (FQDN) by appending more DNS information. Another example is that SMTP specifies that a Date: header must be present in all messages whereas an OFMIP server adds a Date: header to messages that do not have one.

In general, SMTP is used for two purposes: receiving email from other servers and receiving email from mail-composing software (such as Apple's Mail, Microsoft's Outlook, Mozilla's Thunderbird, or Qualcomm's Eudora). Old mail-composing software frequently does not correctly use SMTP. Because it is so forgiving, an

OFMIP server is a convenient approximation of SMTP for injecting mail into an SMTP server (such as qmail), particularly from such clients. However, when receiving email from other servers, it is generally better to enforce the SMTP protocol more strictly.

Included in the mess822 package (`http://cr.yp.to/mess822.html`) is a program that provides an OFMIP service, and functions (more or less) as a drop-in replacement for `qmail-smtpd`. The program is called `ofmipd`. It is not a general-purpose replacement for `qmail-smtpd` because it is too forgiving and does not enforce most of the restrictions that the SMTP protocol requires. In addition to adding Date: headers, correcting email addresses, and allowing a host of other sloppy behaviors, `ofmipd` corrects and accepts all email. Thus, if it were to be used in place of `qmail-smtpd` for SMTP reception, it would provide an open relay that spammers could use to send mail through the system.

Summary

In this chapter, we took a look at how to inject and queue email in the qmail architecture. Next we will examine the output end of the qmail email architecture.

3
Getting Email Out of the Queue

This chapter covers the output end of the qmail mail system, or how email is delivered by qmail and how it leaves the message queue. The following figure describes this part of the overall structure of qmail described in Chapter 1.

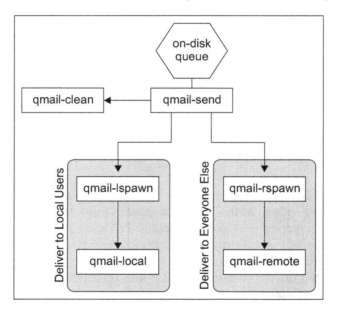

qmail-send and the Qmail Queue

The primary function of the on-disk queue is to serve as a reliable storage and signaling mechanism for the `qmail-send` program, which is the heart of the qmail queuing system. The `qmail-send` program's most fundamental task is to make the primary routing decision: whether a given email should be delivered locally or remotely. This decision is made exactly once per recipient, and is stored in the queue with the email.

The `qmail-send` program can be thought of as a military general, commanding the qmail delivery army. As a general, it has two sergeants: `qmail-lspawn` and `qmail-rspawn`. Depending on whether a given email should be delivered locally or remotely, delivery commands for that email are given to either `qmail-lspawn` (for local deliveries) or `qmail-rspawn` (for remote deliveries). Like `qmail-send`, these two programs make key decisions and then delegate responsibility to the foot soldiers of the qmail delivery army: `qmail-local` and `qmail-remote`. The `qmail-send` program limits the concurrency of deliveries performed by `qmail-lspawn` and `qmail-rspawn`, according to the content of the control files `control/concurrencyremote` (defaults to 20 concurrent deliveries) and `control/concurrencylocal` (defaults to 10 concurrent deliveries).

Determining whether an address is local or remote is based on two control files: `control/locals` and `control/virtualdomains`. The `control/locals` file is a list of local domains, one per line. Any address whose host part (after the @ symbol) is listed in `control/locals` is considered local. The `control/virtualdomains` file specifies patterns that will match against domains, domain-suffixes, and users at specific domains. Any address matching a pattern in the `control/virtualdomains` file is considered to be a virtual address. Virtual addresses are handled in a manner similar to local addresses — they are not relayed to another machine and are delivered locally.

Once an email is delivered, either remotely or locally, it is removed from the on-disk queue by `qmail-clean` at the behest of `qmail-send`. If any messages fail to be delivered (in a *temporary* way, for example if the destination server could not be contacted), the `qmail-send` program retries sending them according to an exponential back-off schedule. If a message remains in the queue for too long, or was permanently rejected during delivery, `qmail-send` creates a bounce message to be sent to the original message's sender.

Delivering Email Locally

The `qmail-lspawn` program is given delivery commands for local messages. Each delivery command consists of a message number, a sender, and a recipient. It uses first the qmail-users mechanism and, if necessary, the `qmail-getpw` program (the qmail interface to UNIX system users) to locate the home directory and other relevant details about each recipient. Then `qmail-lspawn` spawns a `qmail-local` instance to deliver to that user. The `qmail-local` instance is spawned asynchronously, so the actual deliveries can occur in any order. In order to execute deliveries safely and securely, the `qmail-local` program must run with the UNIX **User Identification Number (UID)** and UNIX **Group Identification Number (GID)** of the recipient. Thus, `qmail-lspawn` must run as the *root* user, so that when spawning the `qmail-local` program to do the delivery, `qmail-lspawn` can change to the necessary UID.

One thing to note is that because `qmail-lspawn` runs as *root* and `qmail-local` runs as the user to whom the mail is being delivered, `qmail-local` cannot read messages out of the on-disk queue but `qmail-lspawn` can. Thus, part of `qmail-lspawn`'s job is to open the message in the queue and hand it to `qmail-local`.

The Default

When `qmail-lspawn` starts via `qmail-start`, it receives a single argument—a default delivery instruction. This instruction is passed on to each `qmail-local` instance as they are created. In the absence of further delivery instructions, `qmail-local` uses this method to deliver the email it is given. This default instruction can be as complex as a .qmail file; indeed, the default instruction format is identical to the format of the contents of a .qmail file. In a typical install, this default is specified in the `rc` file, which is the script that uses `qmail-start` to set up all of the persistent sending processes (`qmail-send`, `qmail-lspawn`, `qmail-rspawn`, and `qmail-clean`).

.qmail Files

The `qmail-local` program's task is to first locate the correct .qmail file for the recipient and then use that file's contents (or, if there isn't one, the default instructions) as a list of instructions for delivering the email.

The syntax of these files is very simple, but allows for some rather complex behavior. Every line of the .qmail file is either a delivery instruction or a comment. Comments are lines that begin with a hash mark (#).

There are three types of delivery instructions that are processed in the order they appear in the file:

- A forward
- A file or folder to deliver to
- A pipe to a program

Forwards

The first type of delivery instruction is the simplest. To tell qmail to deliver the message to a different address, simply create a line containing only an email address to which it must be delivered. In cases where a given address is confusing, putting an ampersand (&) at the beginning of the line makes it explicit. For example:

```
&user@example.com
```

Extraneous spaces or extra comments cause qmail to complain about malformed delivery instructions. If the new recipient address is a local address, only the account name is necessary.

Maildirs and mboxes

The second type of delivery instruction is also simple, but has a convenient twist. Files and folders can be specified as either full paths or relative paths. A full path begins with a forward slash and a relative path begins with a period. Relative paths are relative from the user's home directory. For example:

```
# This is a full path
/home/user/mailbox
# This is a relative path
./mailbox
```

If these instructions are in the user's .qmail file, two copies of the message are delivered to the mailbox file in the user's home directory. Qmail delivers email in one of the following two formats: mbox and Maildir. A full discussion of the comparative merits of these two formats is given in Chapter 4. For now, it is sufficient to say that an mbox is a single file containing multiple email messages. It is specified in a delivery instruction as any file whose name does not end in a slash. A Maildir is a directory-based mail storage format. It is specified in a delivery instruction as any file whose name ends in a slash. For example:

```
# This is an mbox in the user's home directory
./Mail
# This is a Maildir in the user's home directory
./Mail/
```

Before messages are delivered to a mailbox (either mbox- or Maildir-formatted), qmail tags them with a Delivered-To header indicating the name of the recipient and a Return-Path header, indicating the original envelope sender. Messages delivered to an mbox also receive the mbox-required "From_" header (which is different than the standard From header).

It is important to note that getting rid of email by specifying delivery to /dev/null is not a good idea. The reason for this is that qmail will treat /dev/null as an mbox that needs to be locked (with flock()) before delivery takes place. Unfortunately, according to the POSIX standard, flock() cannot operate on special files like /dev/null. Even if an operating system allows it, this slows down the process of discarding the message, because multiple messages that need to be discarded simultaneously are discarded one at a time. A better way to tell *qmail-local* to discard the email is to create a .qmail file containing only comments. Note that an *empty* .qmail file is treated as if it does not exist (and thus the default delivery instructions are used). However, if the file contains only comments (lines that start with a hash mark), it overrides the default delivery instructions and causes *qmail-local* to discard the email.

Pipes and Programs

The third type of delivery instruction is deceptively simple in appearance. Any line that begins with a vertical bar, also known as a *pipe*, indicates that the rest of the line should be interpreted by /bin/sh and the content of the email provided on standard input.

For example, a simple program that only discards the email (this is not the best way to discard email) is something like this:

```
| cat > /dev/null
```

A common use for this type of delivery instruction is to use a program to create vacation messages. For example, the following delivery instructions deliver the message to a mailbox and create a vacation message:

```
# deliver it
./Mail
# send to the "vacation" program (may not work, see below)
| vacation
```

Unlike what happens when messages are saved to an mbox or Maildir, emails sent to programs in this manner are not prepended with the Delivered-To, Return-Path, or From_ headers. If these headers are needed, use the preline program to add these headers and then send the message to the command specified in its arguments. For example, most vacation programs require the use of the preline program to operate correctly:

```
# generate vacation message
| preline vacation
```

If a delivery program specified in the .qmail file sends anything to standard output, this output is collected and logged in the *qmail-send* log file. For example, the following will save message Subject headers in the log:

```
# log the subject
| grep '^Subject: '
```

Actually, the above instruction will log all lines in the email that start with "Subject:". If, for example, the message contains a forwarded message in its body that also has a Subject header, both will be logged. Another complication is that long subjects are sometimes split into multiple lines, and grep will only report the first line. Instead of grep, a better tool to use for this purpose is the 822field program in the mess822 package (http://cr.yp.to/mess822.html):

```
# log the subject
| 822field Subject
```

The program specified by the delivery instruction doesn't have to do anything with the email it is given. For example:

```
| echo this goes in the log!
```

Environment variables can be used in these commands. Qmail provides several helpful environment variables. For example, the following logs the sender and recipient of messages (this is just an example; that information is part of the standard log):

```
# log the sender and recipient
| echo $SENDER sent a message to $RECIPIENT
```

Qmail provides the following environment variables:

Environment Variable	Description
SENDER	The envelope sender address.
NEWSENDER	The sender used for forwarding messages (i.e. delivery instructions beginning with an ampersand &).
RECIPIENT	The envelope recipient address; local@domain.
LOCAL	The local part of the RECIPIENT address.
USER	The user receiving the message.
HOME	The receiving user's home directory.
HOST	The domain part of the RECIPIENT address.
HOST2	The portion of HOST preceding the last dot. For example, if HOST is server1.example.com, HOST2 will be server1.example.

Environment Variable	Description
HOST3	The portion of HOST2 preceding the last dot, if there is one. From the previous example, HOST3 is server1. However, if HOST is something shorter, like example.com, HOST3 is undefined.
HOST4	The portion of HOST3 preceding the last dot, if there is one.
EXT	The address extension. For example, if LOCAL is user-extension1-extension2, then EXT is extension1-extension2.
EXT2	The second part of the address extension, if there is one, otherwise EXT2 is undefined. From the above example, EXT2 is extension2.
EXT3	The third part of the address extension, if there is one.
EXT4	The fourth part of the address extension, if there is one.
DEFAULT	The part of EXT that matched against a default .qmail filename, if there is one.
DTLINE	The Delivered-To header that may be added to the message.
RPLINE	The Return-Path header that may be added to the message.
UFLINE	The UUCP-style From_ header that may be added to the message.

Commands specified after the pipe symbol can use any syntax that /bin/sh understands, including conditionals and pipes. For example:

```
# sanitize the subject before logging it
| 822field Subject | sed s/unspeakable/____/g
```

Another good example is a script that replaces the behavior of the preline program:

```
# generate vacation message
| ( echo "$UFLINE$RPLINE$DTLINE"; cat - ) | vacation
```

It is important to note that the output of one delivery instruction cannot be used as input to any of the others. Each delivery instruction receives an identical copy of the email. One of the ways to work around this is to use multiple addresses. The first recipient address will receive the message and pipe it to a filter, which will then requeue the message to be delivered to another address, which can do multiple deliveries based on the filtered form of the message. A filter behaving in this manner looks something like the following:

```
# filter and forward
# remove all instances of the word "foo"
| sed s/\<foo\>//g | forward $LOCAL-filtered@$HOST
```

The final twist that makes .qmail files a viable form of mail filtering is the exit code of the programs run. The exit codes of programs called by *qmail-local* are used to control progress through the .qmail file. Specifically, an exit code of 0 indicates a successful delivery, while an exit code of 99 indicates that the mail was delivered successfully but that none of the subsequent delivery instructions should be followed. An exit code of 100 indicates that the delivery failed permanently (i.e. the message was rejected, which prevents the rest of the delivery instructions from being followed), and an exit code of 111 indicates that the delivery failed temporarily and that delivery should be retried later (which also stops progress through the file). This allows for some interesting filtering possibilities:

```
# user2 never has anything good to say
| test $SENDER == user2@example.com && exit 100
# user3 doesn't either, but he gets mad if I reject his emails
| test $SENDER == user3@example.com && exit 99
# do I have enough space?
# (this is unnecessary, and is just for demonstration)
|quota|tail -1|awk '$4 < 90 { print yes }'|grep -q yes||exit 111
# if I make it this far, it's time to deliver my email
./Maildir/
```

Although .qmail-based filtering can be very useful, it can be somewhat awkward for complex filtering. It is often desirable to use a program with a more concise filtering language to filter and deliver mail. The two most common programs that serve this purpose are procmail and maildrop. A basic .qmail file for using procmail would look like the following:

```
| preline procmail ./.procmailrc
```

Using maildrop would be very similar.

Supporting .forward Files

The Sendmail email server has a feature similar to the .qmail file, whereby users can specify that messages addressed to them are forwarded elsewhere. In particular, users can create a file named .forward in their home directory containing a forwarding email address. There is a program that provides some compatibility with this Sendmail feature called dot-forward (http://cr.yp.to/dot-forward.html). The dot-forward program is used in .qmail files or, more usefully, in the default delivery instructions given to *qmail-start*. The dot-forward program does not support the full range of syntax that a modern Sendmail installation allows in the .forward files, but does support the most basic syntax. A .qmail-style syntax that uses the dot-forward command is very simple.

```
| dot-forward
```

Users

Qmail uses a very flexible definition of a *user*. Like most other mail servers, one definition of *user* is operating-system-defined users. In other words, the users specified in the /etc/passwd file (or wherever the operating system stores user information). These users are used by default for the local domains. However, the operating-system-defined users are easily overridden.

A *user*, in the most general sense, is a unique delivery script associated with a unique email address. For example, fred@example.com, fran@example.com, and pat@example.com are all different addresses, and probably refer to different accounts (users): *fred, fran*, and *pat*. The simplest case uses the operating system to define all these accounts.

As a category, *virtual* users are all users that are not defined by the host operating system, but are instead defined either by qmail or by some other program. Qmail has several different forms of virtual users:

- Aliases
- Qmail-defined, or mapped, users
- Users specified in the control/virtualdomains file
- Extensions to existing users

When attempting to deliver a message, qmail decides how to deliver the message by performing the following operations in the order listed:

1. Check control/virtualdomains
2. Check for qmail-defined users
3. Check for operating-system users
4. Check for aliases

During delivery, qmail handles any address extensions.

The virtualdomains File

The first location that can define a user is the control/virtualdomains file. This file is explained in greater detail in Chapter 5, however, to explain it in short, email addresses defined in this file are rewritten to map to another user. The email then continues through the sequence of user lookups to be delivered with this new destination.

Defined Users: The users/assign File

The `users/assign` file is a very powerful tool for controlling delivery rules. It is used to define users specific to qmail, to map these users to other users, and even to change the rules defining extension addresses. This file is compiled into a CDB file to make it extremely quick to look up delivery instructions. For this reason, systems with large numbers of operating-system-defined users frequently put them here to increase the speed of the delivery process by locating the user's home directory and UID/GID faster. Qmail provides a tool for copying users from `/etc/passwd` to `users/assign`, to make this process easy. The tool, *qmail-pw2u*, reads a SysV7-style `/etc/passwd` file from standard input and prints `users/assign` entries for each user to its standard output.

Aliases

After checking the operating-system-defined user list (`/etc/passwd`), if no matching user is found, the aliases are consulted. Aliases are defined by `.qmail` files in the *alias* user's home directory. For example, creating a file in the *alias* user's home directory named `.qmail-someuser` defines an *alias* for the address `someuser@yourdomain.com`. Another example is the *root* alias that was defined in Chapter 1. A file named `.qmail-root` in `~alias/` establishes the address `root@yourdomain.com`. When attempting to deliver messages addressed to `root@yourdomain.com`, qmail first checks the list of users (in `/etc/passwd`). Because it ignores all users whose UID is zero—namely, *root*—it doesn't find a match. Next qmail consults the aliases defined in the home directory of the *alias* user. Upon finding the `~alias/.qmail-root` file, it delivers the message according to the instructions contained therein.

Extensions

One of the more unusual features of qmail email delivery is the *address extension* feature. In a default qmail configuration, the local part of an email address (considering that email addresses are in the form `local@host`) can contain, in addition to an account name, extra information called an *extension* separated from the account name by a hyphen. Extensions are defined by the recipient user with `.qmail` files in that user's home directory.

For example, messages addressed to `user@example.com` will be delivered to the user named *user*. A message addressed to `user-extension@example.com` will be delivered according to the extensions that *user* has defined (presuming there is no user named *user-extension*). What extensions the *user* permits are defined by `.qmail` files in the *user*'s home directory. Delivery instructions for messages addressed to `user@example.com` are listed in a `.qmail` file in *user*'s home directory, specifically `~user/.qmail`. Extensions are defined by adding the extension to the name of the

.qmail file. For example, the file .qmail-foo will define the foo extension, enabling delivery of messages addressed to user-foo@example.com. It is also possible to have wildcard matching, on a prefix-match-only basis. Specifically, the ending -default in a .qmail file name will match anything matching the existing prefix. Using the example of a message addressed to user-foo@example.com, qmail will look for the following files, in the order given:

1. ~user/.qmail-foo
2. ~user/.qmail-default
3. ~alias/.qmail-user-foo
4. ~alias/.qmail-user-default
5. ~alias/.qmail-default

The first one that exists is read by *qmail-local* to get the delivery instructions. Extension resolution can be more complicated. For example, if a message is addressed to user-foo-bar-baz@example.com, qmail looks for the following files, in the order given:

1. ~user/.qmail-foo-bar-baz
2. ~user/.qmail-foo-bar-default
3. ~user/.qmail-foo-default
4. ~user/.qmail-default
5. ~alias/.qmail-user-foo-bar-baz
6. ~alias/.qmail-user-foo-bar-default
7. ~alias/.qmail-user-foo-default
8. ~alias/.qmail-user-default
9. ~alias/.qmail-default

The first of these files that exists is used to deliver the message. If none of them exists, the message is rejected and the original sender is sent a bounce message saying that the message could not be delivered because the specified recipient does not exist. The user identification process—where the local part of the address, user-foo-bar-baz, is resolved to the user named *user*—is performed by *qmail-lspawn*. When *qmail-local* runs, the choice of which user will receive the message has already been made. It is *qmail-local*'s task to identify the correct .qmail file for the address, given the recipient user identified by *qmail-lspawn*.

There are several environment variables that may be defined (listed in the *Pipes and Programs* section), depending on which .qmail file is used to deliver the message. For each of the above cases, if RECIPIENT is user-foo-bar-baz@example.com,

LOCAL is user-foo-bar-baz, and USER is *user*, the relevant environment variables will be defined during delivery as follows:

Matching .qmail file	EXT	EXT2	EXT3	EXT4	DEFAULT
.qmail-foo-bar-baz	foo-bar-baz	bar-baz	baz		
.qmail-foo-bar-default	foo-bar-baz	bar-baz	baz		baz
.qmail-foo-default	foo-bar-baz	bar-baz	baz		bar-baz
.qmail-default	foo-bar-baz	bar-baz	baz		foo-bar-baz

A common misconception is that emails sent to user@example.com will be delivered according to the .qmail-default file in *user*'s home directory. Keep in mind that the -default only matches extensions, not lack of extensions. For the same reason, when delivering a message addressed to user-foo-bar-baz@example.com, *qmail-local* does not check for the file .qmail-foo-bar-baz-default.

Delivering Email Remotely

The *qmail-rspawn* program, similar to *qmail-lspawn*, is given commands to deliver messages. The difference is that the messages *qmail-rspawn* must deliver must be delivered remotely. The *qmail-rspawn* program merely hands the message to *qmail-remote* along with the host to be contacted, the envelope sender, and the envelope recipient. The *qmail-remote* instances are spawned asynchronously, so deliveries can happen in any order. Unlike *qmail-lspawn*, which performs user identification and sets up the environment for *qmail-local*, *qmail-rspawn* functions merely as a launcher for *qmail-remote* that reads messages from the queue.

While *qmail-rspawn* and *qmail-remote* both run as a user (*qmailr*) with permission to read mail out of the qmail queue, they behave similarly to *qmail-lspawn* and *qmail-local*. The *qmail-rspawn* program reads the message from the queue and feeds it to *qmail-remote*.

How It Normally Works

The delivery commands from *qmail-send* consist of only a message number, a sender address, and a recipient address. The *qmail-rspawn* program extracts the destination domain from the recipient address and gives all that information, unmodified, to *qmail-remote*. The *qmail-remote* program performs all of the necessary SMTP-defined behavior to deliver a message: it looks up the DNS MX records for the destination hostname (and if there are none, the DNS A records) to determine what IP address to contact, contacts that IP address, negotiates the delivery, and transmits the message.

Because *qmail-send* limits the number of concurrent deliveries, offline destinations can cause problems. When a given IP address cannot be contacted (for example, because it is offline), *qmail-remote* is required to wait for the usual timeout (configurable via `control/timeoutconnect`) before giving up. Similarly, if a destination goes offline while *qmail-remote* is communicating with it, qmail is required to wait for a different timeout (configurable via `control/timeoutremote`) before giving up. Because of this waiting process, it's possible that all of the allowable concurrency in remote deliveries could be used by *qmail-remote* instances attempting to contact the same offline server. In some cases (such as when the server first goes offline) this is unavoidable. After several failed attempts to contact a server such a situation is avoidable. *qmail-remote* keeps track of servers that it could not contact even after trying twice in two minutes (without intervening successful connections) and prevents further attempts for an hour. This record of offline servers can be cleared manually to force immediate retries by running the *qmail-tcpok* program as *root*.

Static Routes

It is sometimes necessary or desirable to avoid performing DNS lookups to determine which host to contact for a given destination domain. There are several reasons for this like speed (if DNS lookups are slow and the target IP will virtually never change), DNS information for that domain being unavailable, cases where messages must be relayed but where the public DNS information should not be used by this mail server, and so on. For example, if a qmail server is serving as a backup MX server for a given domain, obeying the DNS MX records is likely to produce bad behavior. These records might list additional backup servers, which would cause qmail to send these mails to the other backup servers causing the messages to loop until the primary MX becomes available. Instead, these messages should be sent only to the primary mail server, whenever it comes back online. By specifying the primary mail server for that domain in the `control/smtproutes` file, the correct behavior is achieved.

Static routes are specified in the file `control/smtproutes`, which is read by *qmail-remote* before doing DNS lookups. The format of this file is a series of entries, one per line, in one of the following two forms: `domain:relay` or `domain:relay:port`. In this form, `domain` is the domain that is being redirected and `relay` is the hostname (or square bracketed IP address) to deliver that domain's mail to. The `port` allows the specification of a port number to use other than the SMTP default port of 25. For example, if the file contains:

```
example.com:realdomain.com
example2.com:[1.2.3.4]
example3.com:anotherdomain.com:26
```

This means that if a message is addressed to `user@example.com`, it is delivered to `realdomain.com`, as if `example.com`'s only MX record specified `realdomain.com`. If a message is addressed to `user@example2.com`, it is delivered to the IP address `1.2.3.4`, and if a message is addressed to `user@example3.com`, `qmail-remote` delivers the message to `anotherdomain.com`, but will contact that server on port 26 rather than the usual port 25.

It is possible to use prefix wildcards in this file by using a line that begins with a period. The longest match in the file will be used. For example:

```
.example.com:[1.2.3.4]
.com:[1.2.3.5]
```

This specifies that all domains ending in `.example.com`, such as `foo.example.com` and `bar.example.com` (but not `badexample.com`, or `example.com`) must be delivered to the IP address `1.2.3.4`. Other messages whose destination ends in `.com` will be delivered to the IP address `1.2.3.5`. Also, a catch-all entry may be specified by omitting the matching domain entirely. For example:

```
:mail.isp.com
```

This tells `qmail-remote` to deliver all messages, regardless of their destination, to the mail server of `mail.isp.com`. Additionally, the relay part of a line can be omitted, specifying that matching destinations should be delivered normally. This is useful for specifying exceptions, for example:

```
example.com:
:mail.isp.com
```

This specifies that all mail destined for `example.com` should be delivered according to the `example.com` DNS records, while all other mail should be relayed through the `mail.isp.com` email server. The routes listed in the file can have only one match. In other words, to direct `example.com` email somewhere, only one line (the first one found) may be used. Each route can only list a single hostname or IP address. If multiple potential destinations are required, keep in mind that hostnames may resolve to multiple IP addresses.

Authentication

When relaying messages through another server, in some circumstances it is useful to authenticate oneself to that other server. There are many ways of authenticating to a remote server, including authenticating with SSL certificates and authenticating with a username and password. Unfortunately, qmail does not support any such behavior natively.

This functionality can be added to qmail either with a patch written by Bjoern Kalkbrenner:
(`http://www.cyberphoria.org/?display=projects_qmail_smtp_auth_send_patch`) or with a patch based on that written by Dr. Erwin Hoffmann
(`http://www.fehcom.de/qmail/auth/qmail-authentication-067_tgz.bin`).
Both patches introduce a new control file, `control/smtproutes_users`, whose syntax is similar to that of `control/smtproutes`. Entries are lines in the file of the form:

```
user@domain:relay|username|password
```

The most common use of this file is in relaying all messages to a server that requires authentication, such as a service provider's server. Similar to `control/smtproutes`, omitting the part before the first colon creates an entry that matches all messages. If all messages must be relayed through the `mail.isp.com` server, with the username *myaccount* and the password *bigsecret*, the `control/smtproutes_users` entry would be:

```
:mail.isp.com|myaccount|bigsecret
```

Summary

This chapter has explained both primary ways in which email exits qmail's queue and is delivered. All of the major facets of delivery were covered, including what happens when delivery fails, how delivery can be filtered with `.qmail` files, how users are defined, and how to control remote delivery. The next chapter will cover local delivery in greater detail, focusing on storage formats and popular methods of accessing email.

4
Storing and Retrieving Email

Along with sending and reading email, one of the most popular things to do with email is to store it. The requirements for storing email tend to change over time; sometimes on-disk efficiency is extremely important, sometimes access time, sometimes reliability in a particular environment, or the ability to search through all messages quickly, or something else entirely. There are multiple ways of storing email, each with strengths and weaknesses that make them appropriate for different situations.

Popular Storage Formats

In addressing these different requirements, several ways of storing email (*storage formats*) have become popular. One of the oldest and least well defined is known as mbox. An mbox-formatted mailbox is a single file containing several messages concatenated together. There are several varieties of mbox formats, and the distinctions between them are primarily in the way each email is distinguished from the next, though there are other differences. One of the biggest drawbacks of this approach is that modifying or deleting messages that are stored in the middle (or at the beginning) of a large mailbox requires rewriting the entire mbox file. If the mailbox is large, this can take a significant amount of time. Another drawback of the mbox format is that the mailbox file must be locked before it can be modified. In some circumstances, like when the mbox is stored on an NFS drive, locking can be unreliable. In other circumstances, such as high-volume mailboxes, forcing all deliveries to be done serially slows delivery speed dramatically.

The storage format used by the MH Message Handling System, known as MH folders, attempts to address some of mbox's problems. Unlike an mbox, where all messages are stored in a single file, MH stores each message in a separate file in a single directory. This improves upon one of the most significant mbox problems by allowing any message to be deleted or modified without touching the rest of the messages. Thus, even very large collections of messages can be modified quickly.

This, of course, relies on the efficiency of the underlying filesystem for storing directory information and handling many open/close operations. However, like mbox, deliveries to an MH folder must use a lock to prevent multiple messages from being delivered to new files with the same name.

Another storage format, Maildir, was invented by Dr. Bernstein and has gained both popularity and acceptance by virtually all other major mail-server software. Like an MH folder, Maildir stores each message in a unique file. Unlike an MH folder, the name of each new file must be formatted in a way that avoids having multiple Maildir-compliant delivery agents attempting to deliver to the same file (though they must still check for the destination file's existence to guard against error). Additionally, the Maildir format specifies that each Maildir folder consists of three sub-folders, one for temporary storage of messages while they are being delivered (`tmp`), one for completely delivered new message files (`new`), and one for everything else (`cur`). This allows operations like checking for new messages to be very quick, and prevents half-delivered emails from being treated as readable, delivered messages if the delivering system crashes during delivery.

One of the other ways in which mail is commonly stored is in a custom database. This method offers the possibility of much more efficient storage and retrieval than is usually experienced on a standard filesystem. However, it generally becomes equivalent to a custom filesystem with special mail-based metadata. Using a custom database usually involves custom indexing that can make searching through the collection of mails very fast. On the other hand, storing mail in a database is extremely easy to do badly (such as by using an unmodified SQL database).

There are many more storage formats, as many mail software packages have either invented their own or modified one of the more mainstream formats to suit the purposes of their mail client. Some mail software packages even combine the storage formats for one reason or another. No single storage format is universally better than all other solutions for all situations. To evaluate these formats for a given situation, or to evaluate some new storage mechanism, one must understand the basic requirements of the mail storage for that situation and the features each storage solution provides. While there are many more things that may be required of a mail-storage technique, the basics are explained here.

Qmail supports only the mbox and Maildir formats natively. The MH format is included in this discussion for context and to help illustrate the benefit and intent of various details of the design of the Maildir format. There is a backwards-compatible extension to the original Maildir specification: Maildir++. This, among other things, provides greater filename collision avoidance on systems that can re-use **Process Identifiers (PIDs)** multiple times in the same second. There is a patch to qmail (`http://www.shupp.org/patches/qmail-maildir++.patch`) written by Bill Shupp that makes qmail use the Maildir++ specification.

Reliability

Perhaps the most important feature that a mail storage system must provide is reliability. Ordinary operations, even at high speed, should not corrupt mailboxes. Additionally, it is usually desirable for the format to survive even unexpected problems, such as power outages or a software crash. Poor crash survival is one of the problems faced by many forms of mail storage: if the power goes out in the middle of delivering a message, that message may be only partially delivered. While a crash-resistant filesystem might prove helpful by preventing unfinished file operations from being committed to disk, it does not help when one is restricted to certain environments. For example, one may need to store emails on a network filesystem like NFS or Samba/CIFS. If the delivering agent crashes mid-delivery, the message is only partially delivered, and the network filesystem cannot tell the difference.

Most mbox-based storage formats have, among other problems, the problem of reliability. If the first message in an mbox has been removed, the full mbox must be rewritten to disk. During this process it is extremely vulnerable to crashes: a crash while rewriting the whole mbox will essentially delete every message that hasn't yet been rewritten. The larger the mbox, the more vulnerable it becomes. This, however, isn't the biggest vulnerability of mbox mailboxes, and can be avoided by using temporary files. More worrying is the problem of partial delivery. If delivery fails and leaves a partial message at the end of the mailbox, the next message to be delivered is considered to be part of the partial message. However, if the circumstances of using the mail collection require read-only access, these problems are entirely mitigated and some of mbox's strengths (such as extremely efficient storage of email) may make it the best tool for the job.

The entire mbox file is vulnerable to a crash or power outage while it is being modified; simply splitting the messages as an MH folder does, only limits the problem. MH folders being modified during a crash are vulnerable to partial or corrupted messages, rather than partial or corrupted mailboxes, because there is no visible distinction between a partially delivered message and a completely delivered message. If the power goes out while a message is being delivered or modified, all unwritten portions of the message may be destroyed (rather than all unwritten portions of the entire mailbox). If the mail system recognizes that the message wasn't successfully delivered and retries delivery later, there will be duplicate messages in the MH folder where one version of the message is only partial and the other is complete.

Both these problems may also be mitigated by the underlying filesystem to some extent. Saving a file to disk generally involves three to four steps:

1. Opening and/or creating the file
2. Writing the contents of the file
3. Running `fsync()` on the file (optional)
4. Closing the file

The fundamental problem arises because, to improve speed, files are frequently not actually written to the disk when programs expect them to be. Instead, they are cached, and written to the disk whenever it is convenient for the operating system. If the system crashes before the file is actually written to disk, all unwritten portions of the file will vanish. The `fsync()` call tells the operating system to flush all unwritten portions of the file to the disk, though the disk itself may not actually write that file to permanent storage immediately. Journaling filesystems prevent file operations that were not flushed to disk before a crash from appearing once the system has recovered; thus, messages will either be fully delivered or will not appear. Some network filesystems like AFS only consider files to be truly saved to disk once they have been closed (i.e. finished), which achieves roughly the same behavior.

The Maildir format attempts to address the problem of unexpected crashes and power outages without relying on unusual filesystem behavior by making a basic assumption. It relies on the safety (i.e. atomicity) of directory operations; and on most UNIX filesystems, this is a valid assumption to make. Directory operations are typically flushed to disk immediately. When a message is delivered to a Maildir, it is first written into the temporary directory (`tmp`), then once it has been fully written, closed, and sync'd, it is moved into the new mail directory (`new`). As long as renaming files can be done safely, as on many filesystems, this prevents partial messages from appearing in the `new` directory. Similarly, the most common modifications to messages that mail readers make are modifications to the flags of messages: read, forwarded, replied, etc. Rather than modifying the content of the message to reflect changes in flags (as mbox and MH folders require), the message files are merely renamed to reflect these changes—which is safe as long as renaming is safe. Renaming is safe as long as it is essentially atomic: it either did not happen, or did (in other words, a file cannot be partially renamed). On many filesystems, this is indeed true. Some filesystems, however, do not guarantee that renaming is atomic, (for example, by caching the change to write to disk later) which can make Maildir vulnerable to losing messages that had been marked as fully delivered.

Speed

Another major consideration for mail storage formats is the speed with which the necessary operations can be performed on them. The basic operations that tend to be performed on a collection of email are as follows:

- Reading
- Marking (as read/forwarded/replied/flagged/etc.)
- Deleting
- Delivering
- Searching

Reading

Each mail storage format has different speed strengths. For example, mbox files are easy to read linearly, starting at the beginning and going to the end, without jumping back and forth within the file. This makes reading out all the messages from an mbox extremely fast. Comparatively, reading multiple messages from both MH folder and Maildir storage formats requires opening, reading, and closing many files in quick succession. On most operating systems, opening a file is more time-consuming than simply reading the next block in an already-open file. So both MH folders and Maildirs can take significantly longer than mbox files to read in full. There is a slight difference if one already knows which message one needs: if only one file needs to be opened, MH and Maildir are just as fast as mbox. In fact, in some cases, MH and Maildir can be even faster. For example, if one already knows the filename of the message in the Maildir or MH folder, one can merely open that message. Finding the same message in an mbox file requires either the knowledge of the message's offset within the file, or requires starting at the beginning of the file and reading through it sequentially to find the desired message. For this reason, random access to messages in MH and Maildir formats is essentially at the same speed as linear access, while random access in an mbox file typically has a speed penalty.

Marking

Mbox and MH folders store message status information (read, forwarded, replied, flagged, etc.) in a header within the content of the stored message. Modifying this header requires modifying the content of the file containing the message, and thus generally requires the file to be rewritten. On single-message mail collections, this takes the same amount of time for both mbox and MH formats. As the number of messages in the mailbox increases, the amount of time required to alter a flag of a message in an mbox also increases. The amount of time required to modify a message in an mbox may vary greatly, depending on the position of the message to be modified within the file. Maildir, on the other hand, stores most marking information in the name of the file containing the message rather than within the file itself, and so does not need to rewrite the entire file, but merely rename it. Depending on the filesystem, this can be extremely fast. Some filesystems (such as FFS and EXT2) store the contents of a directory as merely a list, and modifications require iterating through the list sequentially: the larger the number of messages in the directory, the longer it might take (much like an mbox, the time to find an entry depends on its position in the directory list). Other filesystems store the contents of a directory as a hash (such as EXT3 with the dir_index feature enabled), or as a binary search tree (such as ReiserFS), which makes the process of finding the correct directory entry very quick even in directories containing an extremely large number of files.

Deleting

Deleting messages in mbox files, much like marking a message, requires rewriting of the entire mailbox file to disk, and so can take a long time. In an MH folder and a Maildir, deleting a message is as quick as deleting a file, which is usually very fast.

Delivery

Delivering messages to a mail collection can be much faster than other mailbox modifications. In an mbox, adding a message merely requires appending to the mbox file, which is usually very quick. In MH folders and Maildirs, a new file must be created and then written to, which may take a little longer than appending to an mbox file. The Maildir and MH designs stand out primarily under high-load situations. Mbox files cannot have multiple messages in the process of delivery at the same time: they must be fully written one at a time. Mail delivery programs generally use a locking mechanism of some kind to prevent multiple processes from modifying the mbox file at the same time. MH folders do not suffer from the same problem: multiple processes may deliver and modify messages at the same time, but may not add or delete filenames at the same time. Each file in an MH folder must be named with a sequence number. Mail delivery requires first selecting a sequence number, then checking if it exists already, then exclusively creating it, and possibly repeating the process if a file with the selected name already exists. To prevent conflicts, there is usually a lock involved that allows a sequence number to be safely selected in a single attempt. Maildir removes even this restriction, and allows as much parallelism as the underlying filesystem can support. New messages are placed in files that have names with a specific format that makes naming collisions exceedingly unlikely, and if there is a collision, waiting and trying again a single time is usually all that is necessary to resolve the conflict. While on most filesystems file creation is still a serial action, the benefit of Maildir is that no lock must be used, which makes Maildir safe to use in situations where file locking is unreliable or unavailable (such as on some NFS implementations).

Searching

Searching through messages has become one of the most focused-on areas for improving mail storage performance. In large collections of messages, identifying the ones from a particular sender or referencing a particular topic is frequently very useful. Unfortunately, these file storage formats do not include specifications of quick indexing methods. At its most basic, searching for a given sender or subject or word in the content of a message requires reading sequentially through each message and parsing the headers and body in search of the desired data. Mbox files, MH folders, and Maildirs offer no inherent advantage beyond the already explored variations in the speed of reading through the entire mail collection. It is this problem that frequently makes mail storage in an SQL database seem attractive, as SQL databases are known for their indexing and rapid searching. The same techniques, however, can be applied to mbox, MH folder, and Maildir storage formats. Creating similar indexes of the features of the messages in each can drastically accelerate searching through them, as long as each feature (sender, subject, etc.) can be associated with a method of quickly finding the related message. Each mailbox format has a method of uniquely identifying and quickly locating the messages within it. A message in an MH folder or Maildir can be identified and quickly located by its filename within the folder. Messages within mbox files can be identified by their offset within the file. Perhaps the only major drawback of adding indexing features to these formats is the overhead of maintaining the indexes as the folders are modified.

On-Disk Efficiency

Mail storage formats are also generally compared by their storage requirements. It is easy to assume that the storage requirements of a given set of emails will be roughly the same regardless of the format in which they are stored, but this is usually a poor assumption.

When messages are stored one-per-file as in an MH folder or a Maildir, they can require much more space on disk than they would if stored in a single file. For example, many simple filesystems have a basic block size of 4 KB (4096 bytes). In other words, disk space is allocated in chunks of 4096 bytes, so an email message that is 200 bytes long will require just as much disk space as email messages 4000 bytes long. A message that is 4097 bytes long requires twice as much space as a message that is 4096 bytes long, if they are stored one per file. More than that, there is overhead in the organization of the files on disk. Multiple files in a directory take more space than a single file because they require multiple entries in the directory's index (though this overhead is frequently minuscule). Additionally, on most modern filesystems each file is associated with some invisible metadata referred to as its **inode**, which takes up at least an extra block on disk. Thus, the impact of a 200-byte message stored in its own file is one 4 KB block for its own data and another 4 KB block for its inode: 8192 bytes must be allocated just to store a single 200-byte message. Some filesystems mitigate this problem somewhat by allowing basic blocks to be fragmented into smaller sizes, (1 KB or 500 bytes or similar). The extent to which this overhead affects a given Maildir or MH folder depends on the size of the messages, the block size of the underlying filesystem, and the ability of the underlying filesystem to fragment blocks.

In contrast to the one-file-per-message storage, mbox files do not suffer from such overhead. Each message is appended directly to the end of the preceding message, requiring less than a block of wasted space per mailbox file (plus the space of the file's inode). The per-message overhead is merely a few bytes to distinguish one message from another.

The POP3 and IMAP Protocols

Email was first introduced long before personal computers became popular, and most email was read from the same central computer on which it was stored. With the advent of the Internet and the widespread use of personal computers, it became much more common for email to be fetched from a central server and read by a client on a personal computer. As SMTP is a sending-based protocol, new communication protocols were devised for fetching mail from the central servers. The most popular are known as the **Post Office Protocol 3** (**POP3**) and the **Internet Mail Access Protocol** (**IMAP**).

POP3 is a very simple protocol with limited capabilities. With it, a client can request messages, delete messages, and detect new messages. However, that is essentially the extent of its feature set. Most POP3 mail clients use POP3 to retrieve the messages and store them locally, then either delete them from the central server or leave them there as a backup copy. Because the protocol is so simple, POP3 servers tend to be extremely lightweight and are frequently used on heavily loaded mail servers that do not have the resources to support more complex protocols. Qmail comes with an example POP3 server, `qmail-pop3d`.

IMAP is a far more complex protocol that makes it easy to manipulate mail messages that are stored on the server. IMAP servers understand standard mail flags (replied, forwarded, read, etc.), folders, searching, out-of-order simultaneous commands, simultaneous connections, MIME decomposition, message headers, message tagging, and more. IMAP clients generally leave mail messages on the server, though they frequently also keep local copies as a cache of the state of the server. Because the protocol is so comprehensive and the server can be commanded by users to perform complex tasks, IMAP servers are frequently rather large and resource-intensive. For this reason, extremely busy mail servers often do not support IMAP.

Protocol and Server Selection

Selecting a protocol to support is not always possible: which to support is frequently a requirement rather than a choice. When it is a choice, the usual deciding factor is the predicted load that the decision will place on the server. IMAP clients typically stay connected for hours at a time; one must predict how many users will be connected at the same time, and whether the server hardware and operating system can handle that number of concurrent clients. An important detail of that answer is how many users are likely to be actively manipulating their email at any one time: the more activity, the more will be required of the CPU and storage system. Additionally, the system must not only be able to support the IMAP server load, but also the load from any other services the system is expected to provide as well, such as SMTP support, spam analysis, and other services both related and unrelated to email. Much of the work in estimating the load depends on the choice of server software and supported features as well as the choice of protocol, making it difficult to estimate in the general case. As server hardware gets more and more capable, however, support for large volumes of IMAP users becomes easier to provide. If the server hardware cannot support an IMAP server at acceptable performance levels, POP3 is the obvious alternative.

Once a protocol has been selected, server software to support that protocol must be selected. The choice of software must necessarily be a balance of many factors such as security, ease of setup and maintenance, compatibility with the mail system back end, speed, hardware requirements, software requirements, and so forth, all depending on the needs and requirements of the system being constructed. If the server will need to support POP3, the qmail POP3 server is probably the most appropriate, as it is simple, secure, fast, and integrates well with anything that can integrate with the rest of qmail. If the server will need to support IMAP, the choice becomes slightly murkier, and frequently involves some degree of personal preference on the part of the administrator. The most popular options include:

- UW-IMAP (http://www.washington.edu/imap/)
  - Pro: It is the canonical IMAP server.
  - Con: It does not support Maildir mailboxes without a patch, and can be difficult to integrate into a qmail-centric system.
- Courier-IMAP (http://www.courier-mta.org/)
  - Pro: Supports Maildir, Maildir++, and a sufficiently large number of authentication mechanisms to be able to integrate with most qmail-based systems.
  - Con: Complex to set up and administer. Resource intensive.
- Dovecot (http://www.dovecot.org/)
  - Pro: Similar feature set to Courier-IMAP, but is simpler to configure and integrate with qmail. Very fast.
  - Con: Young project undergoing rapid development.
- Cyrus IMAP (http://cyrusimap.web.cmu.edu/)
  - Pro: Large array of speed enhancements for fast text searching, many features for extremely large segmented user space and storage, easy virtual domains, and more.
  - Con: Extremely complex. Difficult to integrate with qmail; relies on unique storage format.
- BincIMAP (http://www.bincimap.org/)
  - Pro: Designed to work just like *qmail-pop3d*, extremely simple to integrate with qmail.
  - Con: Has far fewer and more basic features than other servers.

In general, choose a server that provides the required features, and learn how it works. Starting with something simple, like BincIMAP, is a good first step. Keep in mind that if requirements change, the software can always be swapped out.

qmail-pop3d Server Setup

Presuming that qmail is already installed, installing `qmail-pop3d` is a relatively simple task. `qmail-pop3d` requires checkpassword-compliant authentication. The standard SMTP-AUTH patches to qmail also use checkpassword-compliant authentication, so you may have set it up already. The `qmail-popup` program uses the checkpassword interface, which uses pipes to communicate authentication information (username and password) to a small authentication program. This auxiliary program decides whether to accept the user's credentials or not. Once a checkpassword-compatible authentication program is installed and working, `qmail-pop3d` can be run similarly to `qmail-smtpd`. Like `qmail-smtpd`, `qmail-pop3d` can be run from anything that will handle the network connections for it, such as `inetd` or `tcpserver`.

The Checkpassword Interface

Checkpassword is a generic authentication interface (`http://cr.yp.to/checkpwd/interface.html`) designed by Dr. Bernstein. The essential idea is to separate the program performing authentication from the program requesting authentication. This allows the authentication program (which needs to be audited very thoroughly) to be small and entirely separate from the—possibly less trustworthy—program being authenticated. The design also allows the simplest of programs, including shell scripts, to use the authentication program. A checkpassword-compliant authentication program receives credentials (username, password, and a time stamp) in a standard format via file descriptor three and uses its return value to indicate whether the authentication succeeded. A return value of zero indicates success and non-zero indicates failure. Additionally, a checkpassword-compliant authentication program takes as arguments the name and arguments of a program to be run. If authentication succeeds, the specified program is run as the authenticated user, in that user's home directory. In concept, this feature is akin to the program `su - -c`.

Credentials are passed to the checkpassword-compliant authentication program as three null-terminated strings via file descriptor three: first the username, then the password, and then a timestamp (which is usually ignored). For example, the following string could authenticate a user named *user* with the password password: `user\0password\0Y123456\0`.

Note that the \0 indicates a null character, and Y123456 is a generic timestamp. Using a basic checkpassword program (such as checkpassword), the following shell command would print out the authenticated user's home directory when run as *root*:

```
printf "user\0password\0Y123456\0" | checkpassword pwd 3<&0
```

And the following shell command would print out the user's group memberships:

```
printf "user\0password\0Y123456\0" | checkpassword groups 3<&0
```

Installing the checkpassword Program

There are many checkpassword-compatible programs available, supporting a wide variety of authentication mechanisms, all of which are simple and tend to be very easy to compile. Links to many of these programs can be found at http://qmail.org. The most basic, which authenticates standard UNIX users, is the reference implementation, available at:
http://cr.yp.to/checkpwd/checkpassword-0.90.tar.gz

Once the tarball has been downloaded, decompress it as follows:

```
gunzip checkpassword-0.90.tar.gz
tar -xf checkpassword-0.90.tar
```

Then go into the newly created directory and compile the software:

```
cd checkpassword-0.90
make
```

Finally, install it. Sufficient permissions to install it will be required, so this may need to be performed as the *root* user:

```
make setup check
```

Running with tcpserver

Just like *qmail-smtpd*, *qmail-pop3d* can be run from tcpserver and monitored by daemontools. As such, it will need a directory (e.g. /var/qmail/supervise/pop3d) and run file for the daemontools' supervise process to run. An example run file looks like this:

```
#!/bin/sh
exec tcpserver -R -l 0 -H 0 pop3 \
    /var/qmail/bin/qmail-popup FQDN \
    /bin/checkpassword \
    /var/qmail/bin/qmail-pop3d mail 2>&1
```

In this example, the FQDN in the third line must be replaced with the fully qualified domain name of the computer hosting the POP3 server. What this does is tell tcpserver to run the *qmail-popup* program, which does two things:

1. Retrieves authentication information from the client using part of the POP3 protocol.
2. Feeds that information to the checkpassword program.

The checkpassword program:

1. Checks the authentication credentials.
2. If the credentials are valid, changes to the authenticated user's home directory.
3. Sets the correct environment variables for that user (namely, HOME and USER).
4. Runs *qmail-pop3d* as that user.

The *qmail-pop3d* server:

1. Looks for a Maildir-formatted directory named mail in the current directory (the authenticated user's home directory).
2. If it is found, it provides the client access to that mailbox via the POP3 protocol commands.

After the primary run file is set up, set up the logging for the *qmail-pop3d* server. In order to do this first create a directory for storing the log files (e.g. /var/log/qmail/pop3d), owned by the *qmaill* user. Create a directory named log in the same directory as the above run file, and inside that log directory, create another file named run that looks like the following:

```
#!/bin/sh
exec /usr/local/bin/setuidgid qmaill \
    /usr/local/bin/multilog t \
    /var/log/qmail/pop3d
```

Once all these files and directories are created, make sure the run files are executable:

chmod +x /var/qmail/supervise/pop3d/run

chmod +x /var/qmail/supervise/pop3d/log/run

Finally, tell svscan to use this new set of directories to start the *qmail-pop3d* service:

ln -s /var/qmail/supervise/pop3d /service/qmail-pop3d

The *qmail-pop3d* server can now be controlled and monitored in the same way that the *qmail-smtpd* server is.

Webmail

One of the most popular methods for providing portable access to email is through a web-based email client, commonly referred to as **webmail**. Typical webmail programs are email clients that run on, and are only accessible via, a web server. Their basic functionality is the same as that of an email client running on the user's personal machine. As such, they usually use either IMAP or, less commonly, POP3 protocols to fetch the user's email. This not only provides the ability to put the web server (and webmail software) on a computer without direct access to the mail storage (and makes it possible to change the back end without changing the webmail software), but also standardizes the authentication mechanism. The webmail software will simply authenticate via IMAP or POP3 rather than needing to perform user authentication itself. In some cases, webmail software can be packaged with other mail software to give it direct access to the mail storage. This is often done in the name of improved speed, but is not, however, typical.

The most common complaints about webmail are those regarding its speed and its interface. Unlike common mail client programs, webmail is typically restricted to the standard interface components available to most web pages such as clickable links, checkboxes, pop-up menus, radio-buttons, and so forth. Unfortunately, this frequently feels awkward to users accustomed to desktop-based mail-reading software. The advent of **Asynchronous JavaScript and XML (AJAX)** programming has enabled web-based applications, including webmail, to emulate the interface of desktop applications. While generic AJAX webmail applications have not yet become as widespread as the more traditional webmail applications, this is likely to happen within the next several years, and should largely address most complaints about webmail interfaces compared to desktop mail clients. Even AJAX, however, cannot do everything that desktop-based mail programs can, such as integration with other desktop applications.

The other major complaint about webmail—namely, about its speed—can have many causes, only some of which can be mitigated. One reason webmail may be slow, particularly compared to desktop programs, is that it typically cannot take advantage of some of the optimizations that a desktop application can, such as caching messages, and communicating with the IMAP server only when something changes. Web-based applications can typically maintain only a small amount of temporary state information, which means that they cannot cache messages and cannot maintain long-term connections to the mail server. Indeed, many webmail applications must re-authenticate themselves to the mail server for every new web page that the client visits; and usually every operation a user wishes to perform involves loading a new page. This performance can be improved in some cases through the use of a caching IMAP proxy (obviously, only applicable when the webmail application is using IMAP) that maintains long connections and as such can improve the speed of re-authentication.

Because webmail applications usually cannot cache large amounts of data, they rely heavily on the behavior and speed of the underlying IMAP or POP3 mail server. For example, when listing the folders available for storing mail, a client application running on the user's own machine can store the list of mailboxes from the last time it was run, and can thus provide that list instantly and update it later as the server responds with more recent information. Webmail applications, however, cannot store that information from instance to instance, and must always re-request that information from the server. Finally, webmail operations are bound by the capacity of the central server and are subject to the load that the server experiences from multiple users accessing it at the same time. Every webmail action, be it as simple as listing mailboxes or as complex as searching for a pattern in the body of every email, must be performed on the server itself, which is a resource that must be shared by all of the users of the server. Improving the efficiency of either the webmail application or the IMAP or POP3 server upon which it relies can improve webmail speed to some degree, but cannot address the basic problem of sharing a resource among many users.

Summary

This chapter has covered, in depth, the ideas behind storage and retrieval of email. Rather than delving into as much qmail-specific detail as other chapters, this chapter covered many generally important storage topics, including mailbox formats and the two retrieval protocols, POP3 and IMAP. Next up, virtualization!

5
Virtualization

One of the most interesting extensions to the standard mail setup discussed in earlier chapters is that of virtualization. There are many reasons for wanting to virtualize email services, from hosting multiple domains with different users to simply extending the ability to apply policies to different sets of email. There are three basic techniques that are used with a standard qmail system for attaining different forms of virtualization: qmail's `control/virtualdomains` file, user-definable address extensions, and running multiple qmail instances on the same system.

Generic Virtualization Framework

The most straightforward mail handling in qmail is used for what are known as the *local* domains: those listed in the `control/locals` file. The users for these domains are all the same, and are typically the users defined in `/etc/passwd`, though they can be defined in `users/assign` as well (discussed in the *Non-Virtual Non-System Users* section). Qmail, however, has another sense in which an email can be *local*, which is to assign a domain to a user (or, more accurately, to a prefix). This feature is configured with the `control/virtualdomains` file.

Power of the virtualdomains File

The `virtualdomains` file is one of the most powerful, useful, and stunningly simple mechanisms for configuring qmail. Virtual domains and even virtual users can be created, independently of one another, and assigned to controlling users. Virtual domains are fully independent, and as they are assigned to users (or, more accurately, prefixes) they can be in different UNIX protection domains if desired. This file can also define virtual users and similarly assign them to controlling users. This file thus makes it both possible and easy to intercept specific addresses and do something special with them.

Perhaps surprisingly for the power this file wields, the `control/virtualdomains` file is only slightly more complicated than similar control files, such as `control/locals`. Rather than a list of domains, the `virtualdomains` file is a list of patterns and their associated prefixes. The entries are of the form:

matching-pattern: prefix

Only one prefix is associated with each pattern. The matching pattern can be one of the following three things: a domain (that follows the same wildcarding semantics used in the `control/rcpthosts` file), an email address, or an empty string. The empty string is considered to match anything. An email address matches any message addressed to that email address, and a domain matches any message addressed to a user in that domain. If there are multiple possible matches, the longest match is used.

Emails that match patterns listed in the `control/virtualdomains` file are considered to be local emails, similar to those addressed to domains in the `control/locals` file. Messages that match patterns in the `virtualdomains` file must first undergo a simple modification before delivery. While messages are prepared for delivery, if they have an envelope destination address that matches a pattern in the `virtualdomains` file, that destination address is prepended with the matching pattern's associated prefix. This turns the original local part of the address into an extension of the prepended user. In this way a domain can be mapped to a user, giving that user full control over the mailboxes (or users) within that domain. The `virtualdomains` file can also be used to define exceptions to the matching rules, if the prefix is blank.

It is important to note that the `control/virtualdomains` file is considered *after* the `control/locals` file, which means that if an email is addressed to a domain listed in `locals`, the `virtualdomains` file will not apply. Also, `virtualdomains` rewriting occurs *before* the mail is given to `qmail-lspawn` for delivery.

This sounds complex, but is easy to understand with an example.

Basic Virtual Domains

An example `virtualdomains` file that demonstrates most of the file's features is as follows:

```
example.com:foo
.example.com:foo-bar
two.example.com:baz
waldo@domain.com:qux
domain.com:
:garply
```

Presuming that the users mentioned i.e. *foo, baz, qux,* and *garply* are the only local users on this system; these lines cause the following results:

1. The first line matches any address ending in @example.com, such as user@example.com. Such a destination address will be rewritten as foo-user@example.com, ensuring that the email's delivery will be controlled by the local user named *foo*.

2. Messages addressed to user@something.example.com do not match the first line but do match the second line, and so will be delivered as if they had been addressed to foo-bar-user@something.example.com.

3. Because the virtualdomains file is used in a *longest match wins* manner, the third line (not the second) will match messages addressed to user@two.example.com. This destination will be rewritten as baz-user@two.example.com and *baz* will control the delivery of such messages.

4. The fourth line specifies that email addressed to waldo@domain.com will be instead delivered as if it had been addressed to qux-waldo@domain.com. The *qux* user will control that delivery.

5. The fifth line specifies that any domain.com email — other than waldo@domain.com — should be treated as if domain.com had been listed in the control/locals file.

6. Finally, the sixth line specifies that all other email will be rewritten and delivered to the local *garply* user. For example, email addressed to someone@somewhere.org will be rewritten as garply-someone@somewhere.org and delivery will be attempted locally.

In this example, the *foo* user is essentially in charge of the entirety of the example.com domains. Users that are specific to example.com are defined by creating appropriately named .qmail files in *foo*'s home directory.

For example, to establish the standard postmaster@example.com address, *foo* would create a file named .qmail-postmaster in its home directory, containing the instructions for delivering postmaster's email. The *foo* user could also establish a foo@example.com address by creating a file named .qmail-foo in his or her home directory. In this way, once the example.com mapping has been established, the *foo* user can set up and maintain the users in the example.com domain without ever requiring further permission from or contact with the system administrator.

It is worth pointing out that precisely who controls what can get more complex if real usernames have extension separator characters (a hyphen, by default) in them. For example, if the address postmaster@example.com is rewritten to be foo-postmaster@example.com, it is typically delivered according to the instructions in ~foo/.qmail-postmaster or, if that file does not exist, ~foo/.qmail-default.

However, if there is a user named *foo-postmaster*, that user will receive email addressed to `postmaster@example.com`.

If a `.qmail` file (such as `~foo/.qmail-postmaster`) cannot be located for a given extension address (such as `foo-postmaster@example.com`), the *alias* user's directory is checked for `.qmail` files. Specifically, `.qmail-foo-postmaster`, `.qmail-foo-default`, and `.qmail-default`. If none of these files exist, the message is considered undeliverable and is bounced.

Note that during delivery of such an email, the standard environment variables are defined per the rewritten destination rather than per the original address. For example, if a message addressed to `postmaster@example.com` is delivered using the example configuration, the affected environment variables will be defined as follows (assuming *foo*'s home directory is `/home/foo`):

Environment Variable	Content for virtual domain delivery	Content for normal delivery
`RECIPIENT`	`foo-postmaster@example.com`	`postmaster@example.com`
`LOCAL`	`foo-postmaster`	`postmaster`
`USER`	`foo`	`postmaster`
`HOME`	`/home/foo`	`/home/postmaster`
`HOST`	`example.com`	`example.com`
`HOST2`	`example`	`example`
`HOST3`	`example`	`example`
`HOST4`	`example`	`example`
`EXT`	`postmaster`	

The Path of an Email

To better understand how qmail's virtual domain mechanism works, let's attempt to understand it visually. The following chart roughly illustrates the decision-making process that qmail performs when delivering a message (the process starts at the top left):

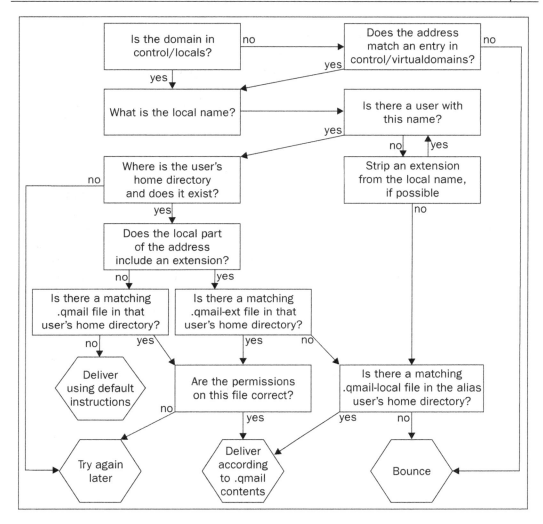

Non-Virtual Non-System Users

To new qmail administrators, the users/assign file is probably the most mysterious file in qmail's configuration. Its purpose is to allow the administrator to define mailboxes (or users) that qmail will treat as potential delivery targets. With this purpose comes the ability to define the name of the .qmail file that will be used to configure the defined user and the way in which that user's extensions will be separated (qmail extensions are typically separated by a hyphen unless changed at compile time in conf-break).

Being able to define mailboxes independent of the underlying operating-system users can be very useful for many purposes. One reason this file is often used is for speed; it is compiled into a CDB-formatted database file, which is faster to read than text, and thus can make the process of looking up users fast. This is particularly valuable in cases when looking up users the usual way (i.e. via getpwent()) is slow—such as when there are very large numbers of users. Being able to create mailboxes independent of the underling operating system can also be used for many creative purposes and organizational schemes. The most popular use of this file, though, is to assist in organizing virtual domains. Each domain can be given its own directory, which may or may not have a unique system user assigned to it.

While this may sound complicated, and the file format is more detailed than any other qmail configuration file, the underlying concept is very simple. For any mailbox, two things are obviously required: a name (i.e. the part of the associated email address to the left of the at @ symbol) and a directory associated with the name. When dealing with users defined by the operating system, this is the username and the user's home directory. Because all files must be owned by a system user of some kind, qmail must know a UID, GID, and username to be used when delivering to this mailbox. For a user (mailbox) defined by the operating system, these are the UID, GID, and username of the user in question, and this same information is defined in the users/assign file. Finally, qmail also allows both the definition of alternative extension separators and an extension to specify the *default* .qmail file in the defined user's home directory. These definitions are compiled into a CDB file—users/cdb— for qmail's use by running the *qmail-newu* program, which must be run whenever the users/assign file is changed.

The /etc/passwd file, which defines UNIX users, generally has a format as follows:

```
username:password:UID:GID:groupname:homedirectory:shell
```

For example:

```
john:x:100:101:doe:/home/john:/bin/sh
```

The users/assign file has most of this same information, but comes in two forms: simple assignments and wildcard assignments. Simple assignments are the easiest, and begin with an equals (=) sign:

```
=mailboxname:username:uid:gid:homedir:dash:ext:
```

The dash and ext parts are concatenated to define a .qmail file for delivery. A simple translation of the above example /etc/passwd user would be something like the following:

```
=john:john:100:101:/home/john:::
```

Note that this provides an alternative method of defining aliases. For example:

```
=zeke:john:100:101:/home/john:::
```

This line will deliver mail sent to *zeke* as if it had been sent to *john*. If *zeke* mail must be sent to the *john* user but must be delivered according to a different .qmail file, a line like this could be used:

```
=zeke:john:100:101:/home/john:-:zeke:
```

This would tell qmail to deliver mail addressed to *zeke* according to the instructions in

```
/home/john/.qmail-zeke.
```

The above example lines are all simple assignments, and do not support extensions. In other words, it will direct email addressed to john@here.com, but not john-test@here.com. That's what wildcard assignments, which begin with a plus (+) sign, are for. Wildcard assignments have the following form:

```
+mailboxprefix:username:uid:gid:homedir:dash:pre:
```

This is essentially equivalent to having an entry for every possible string that could replace EXT:

```
=mailboxnameEXT:username:uid:gid:homedir:dash:extEXT:
```

For example, the following entry will handle john-test@here.com and all similar john-anything@here.com extensions:

```
+john-:john:100:101:/home/john:-::
```

One of the places where this ability to create arbitrary mailboxes can be very useful is in organizing virtual domains. For example, imagine that you are configuring example.com to be a virtual domain. The control/virtualdomains file would have an entry like the following:

```
example.com:example
```

Now that all example.com email will be directed to the example mailbox, the example mailbox must be defined. One way to do this is to have a UNIX user named *example*. Unfortunately, this means that the system will also accept mail addressed to example@yourserver.com (because if *example* is a full UNIX user, it is also a valid recipient). A more restrictive method is to create a wildcard entry in the users/assign file, as follows:

```
+example-:john:100:101:/home/example.com:-::
```

This will make sure that all example.com users are handled by .qmail files in the folder /home/example.com, and that all such messages will be owned by the *john* UNIX user. This also prevents example@yourserver.com from being a valid recipient address.

User-Management Problem in Assisted Virtual Domains

The convenience of having a single user able to configure and manage all of the users for a given virtual domain without the intervention of the system administrator is significant. Unfortunately, managing virtual users even within a single domain is a chore that qmail does not address. Frequently, for example, the users of the domain are defined in a central database containing credentials (passwords), full names, and other associated information, such as is queried by the checkpassword program discussed in Chapter 4. It is sometimes possible to change the user creation, deletion, and modification mechanisms to keep the set of .qmail files for that domain up to date, but such machinations are rarely convenient.

A common method for addressing this problem is simply to create a .qmail-default file in the domain's home directory. This file is then used for the delivery instructions of **all** users in that domain, and can use a script to decide what to do with each message rather than relying on the existence of .qmail files to define that information. The primary benefit of this approach is that users can be defined by virtually any system that can be queried — from an LDAP server to an IMAP server to an SQL database to a flat file to a filesystem — without needing to modify the delivery environment for every change in user information and without needing qmail to support that mechanism.

Popular Solutions: vpopmail and VMailMgr

As managing virtual domains and virtual users is a common frustration, several programs that provide assistance are available. Two of the most popular qmail-compatible ways of managing virtual domains are vpopmail by Inter7 (http://www.inter7.com/index.php?page=vpopmail), and VMailMgr by Bruce Guenter (http://www.vmailmgr.org/). The two are very similar in what they provide.

The way vpopmail works is straightforward. At the basic level, it maintains a database of users (it can use Oracle, Sybase, MySQL, or LDAP databases, or use its own domain-specific CDB files), provides a checkpassword-compliant interface for authenticating against that database, and automatically modifies qmail's configuration files as necessary when domains are added. Each domain has an entry in the control/rcpthosts and control/virtualdomains files, as well as an entry in the users/assign file. The users/assign file is used to give each domain its own home directory without creating a UNIX user for each domain. It can, of course, be told to use different UNIX users for each domain. There is a .qmail-default file in each domain's home directory that feeds email messages to a vpopmail-specific delivery program that verifies the recipient and delivers the email. Additionally, .qmail files in each domain's home directory define aliases or forwards. Each virtual user has a unique home directory within its domain's home directory that can contain user-specific configuration information, such as delivery instructions and spam detection preferences. vpopmail emulates .qmail file handling for these virtual users, so a .qmail file within the virtual user's home directory controls the email delivery for that user. By default, mail is delivered to a Maildir-formatted mailbox named Maildir inside each virtual user's home directory.

For clarity's sake, imagine an email addressed to a vpopmail-managed domain: user@example.com. Imagine that vpopmail has been configured to keep domains in /var/lib/vpopmail/domains/. Here's how delivery would work, from network to disk:

1. First, a remote host contacts the *tcpserver* program listening on port 25—which spawns *qmail-smtpd*—with a message addressed to user@example.com.

2. The *qmail-smtpd* program checks rcpthosts and morercpthosts.cdb and sees example.com listed.

3. The mail is passed to *qmail-queue* by *qmail-smtpd* to be queued on disk.

4. The *qmail-send* program notices the new message in the queue, reads its destination address, and looks for example.com in locals.

5. Not finding it, *qmail-send* next checks in virtualdomains.

6. The virtualdomains entry is:

   example.com:example.com

   So *qmail-send* rewrites the destination address as example.com-user@example.com.

7. The *qmail-send* program commands *qmail-lspawn* to deliver the message.

8. The *qmail-lspawn* program checks the users/cdb file (which was built from users/assign using *qmail-newu*) to see if the example.com user is listed. The relevant entry in users/assign is:

   +example.com-example.com:XXX:YYY:/var/lib/vpopmail/domains/
   example.com:-::

9. The *qmail-lspawn* program spawns a *qmail-local* instance with the information from the users/cdb file.

10. The *qmail-local* program changes to the vpopmail user (user ID number XXX, from the users/cdb file) and enters the /var/lib/vpopmail/domains/example.com/ directory.

11. `qmail-local` sees the `.qmail-default` file in that directory, and reads it.

12. `qmail-local` feeds the message to the only program listed in the `.qmail-default` file: `vdelivermail`.

13. `vdelivermail` checks to make sure that *user* is a registered user of the `example.com` domain.

14. `vdelivermail` checks for a file named `.qmail` in the virtual user's home directory, `/var/lib/vpopmail/domains/example.com/user/`.

15. As there is no `.qmail` file in that directory, `vdelivermail` delivers the message to the Maildir-formatted mailbox, `/var/lib/vpopmail/domains/example.com/user/Maildir/`.

As you can see, it's a complex process.

VMailMgr works very similarly to vpopmail. It also maintains a database of users and passwords in CDB files, and provides both a checkpassword-compliant authentication program and a CourierIMAP module for accessing these files (CourierIMAP supports vpopmail's interface natively). When new domains are added, qmail's configuration files — `rcpthosts` and `virtualdomains` — must be modified manually. Each domain is required to have its own UNIX user and UID, which negates the need to modify the `users/assign` file (though it can be used if desired, to speed looking up user information). The virtual users are organized similarly to vpopmail within each virtual domain's home directory, though there is no emulation of a per-user `.qmail` file. The difference in delivery operations from vpopmail is that *Step 8* becomes a lookup of the `example.com` user in `/etc/passwd`, *Step 10* uses the `example.com` user, *Steps 12* through *15* involve a program called `vdeliver` instead of `vdelivermail`, and *Step 14* doesn't happen.

Consequences for Other Services

Virtual domains are almost always a part of a larger system of storing and retrieving email. Because each virtual user does not have a corresponding UNIX user account, other mail operations must use an abstracted interface such as IMAP or POP3 to securely access a virtual user's mail storage. Additionally, a virtual email domain system also needs to cooperate frequently with other virtual domain systems, such as a virtual web domain system or database system.

There are two facets to cooperating with other virtual domain systems and other related and dependent services. The first is file organization and layout, and the second is user authentication. File organization and layout is the primary consideration during the set up of a new domain: frequently all support files for new domains, regardless of service (email or web or whichever) are collected into a single location or file hierarchy. Though this is usually unnecessary, it has a certain aesthetic appeal, and lends itself to some administrative tasks such as implementing cross-service per-domain disk quotas. On the other hand, it is also sometimes more convenient to separate files by service. For example, mail files tend to be small and may be better served by a different filesystem than web or database files. The home directory qmail will use for each domain can be easily configured using the `users/assign` file or, for management systems like VMailMgr, using `/etc/passwd`. This setup is sufficiently flexible to deal with most rational organization schemes.

Authentication is frequently the most difficult facet of virtual domains to configure because so many different software packages must use it. For example, if virtual domain and virtual user information is stored in a vpopmail- or VMailMgr-specific set of CDB files, getting an IMAP server to authenticate users from these files may be very difficult. The IMAP server must use the checkpassword-style authentication program provided by both packages and be able to understand the user databases without help, or use an intermediary such as the CourierIMAP authentication service that does understand them. If these users are then going to be used by the web server for authentication purposes, the web server must support one of these authentication methods as well. This problem of having multiple services, possibly on different physical computers that need to authenticate from the same set of user data is one of the attractions of service-based authentication mechanisms like LDAP.

Good Reasons to Use Multiple Installations

In some cases, qmail's built-in virtualization support is insufficient to achieve the desired separation between virtual domains. For example, when using the built-in virtualization features the central queue is shared among all of the virtual domains, as is the `qmail-send` process. Because the `qmail-send` process is shared, each of the virtual domains will send outbound email from the same IP address and will have to share remote delivery slots. Because the queue is shared among the virtual domains, all domains must use the same queue management policies, such as the queue lifetime setting, the bounce settings, the double-bounce settings, and so forth.

Virtual domains using the built-in virtualization schemes also frequently share an external IP address and thus share a `qmail-smtpd` server. This forces all the virtual domains to use the same receiving policies as well, such as which (if any) blacklists to use or whether to do SMTP tarpitting or spam- or virus-filtering. Depending on the installation, some of these restrictions can be worked around through creative use of environment variables and wrapper scripts, but it is something that must be worked around in any case. Perhaps the easiest way of giving each domain separate SMTP-server settings — needing a separate SMTP server — is to give each domain a separate IP address and a separate `run` script for each IP address. Thus, settings such as blacklisted IP addresses, filtering, virus scanning, or other SMTP-time activities can be set up on a per-domain basis. Providing each virtual domain with a separate *qmail-smtpd* instance does not, of course, address the limitations of a shared queue and a shared *qmail-send* instance.

In addition to the basic problems associated with virtualization, maintaining multiple qmail installations is useful in any situation where different queue or *qmail-send* settings are desired for some subsection of email. For example, large domains sometimes maintain a separate queue for bounce messages, so that they can be sent out more slowly (i.e. with a lower concurrencyremote setting) or can have a shorter queue lifetime.

Virtualization is not the only reason to use multiple qmail installations, but just one of the most common reasons. Multiple qmail installations are useful in any circumstance where multiple queue policies are necessary, or where central configuration files need to be applied differently in different cases. For example, in order to have two *qmail-smtpd* instances where one behaves as if rcpthosts is empty (i.e. only authenticated users or authorized IP addresses may submit mail) and the other behaves as if rcpthosts has several domains in it, the best solution is to have two qmail installations. The two installations need not have separate queues, though they can.

How to Set Up Multiple Qmail Installations

The crucial detail to setting up and maintaining multiple qmail installations is to alter the conf-qmail file in the qmail source. This file is what defines both where qmail will install its binaries and where those binaries will expect to find each other and their queue. The location of the queue is compiled into the binaries directly, so maintaining a separate queue requires a separate set of binaries.

Assuming that one instance of qmail has already been successfully installed in /var/qmail (the default), a second qmail instance can be installed in (for example) /var/qmail2 by performing the following commands from within the qmail source directory:

```
echo /var/qmail2 > ./conf-qmail
make setup check
```

Once this is done, a new installation of qmail will reside in /var/qmail2. To complete the setup, the appropriate configuration files from /var/qmail/control, such as me, should be copied to /var/qmail2/control. Also, the new *qmail-send* process should be started, (if the new queue will be used) usually with a script nearly identical to that of the original installation.

For example, if the original *qmail-send* process was started with a daemontools `run` script, another `supervise` directory and `run` script for the new *qmail-send* process should be prepared. The second *qmail-send* process is not necessary, if the second qmail installation will share a queue with the first. In that case, all that is necessary is to symlink the *qmail-queue* binary from the first installation into the second (and delete the second's *qmail-queue* binary).

If desired, another `supervise` directory and `run` script may be created to run the new *qmail-smtpd* as well. The trick to get both *qmail-smtpd* instances (the original and this new one) to run together is to specify different IP addresses for them to listen to. The original example script in Chapter 1 specified the arguments to *tcpserver* as follows:

```
tcpserver -R -l "$LOCAL" -H \
    -x /etc/tcp.smtp.cdb \
    -u "$QUID" -g "$QGID" \
    0 smtp \
    /var/qmail/bin/qmail-smtpd 2>&1
```

This — or more specifically, the 0 in the fourth line — specifies that *tcpserver* will listen for SMTP connections on all network interfaces. This prevents other programs, including other *tcpserver* instances, from listening for SMTP connections on any network interface. If, for example, the original qmail installation only needs to listen to the single publicly accessible IP address (for example, 192.168.1.1), then the original setup should be changed to specify that address rather than simply 0. Thus, it would look as follows:

```
tcpserver -R -l "$LOCAL" -H \
    -x /etc/tcp.smtp.cdb \
    -u "$QUID" -g "$QGID" \
    192.168.1.1 smtp \
    /var/qmail/bin/qmail-smtpd 2>&1
```

With the original configuration more specific, the second qmail installation is free to listen to a different address. For example, it could listen to the loopback interface via IP address 127.0.0.1, as follows:

```
tcpserver -R -l "$LOCAL" -H \
    -x /etc/tcp.smtp.cdb \
    -u "$QUID" -g "$QGID" \
    127.0.0.1 smtp \
    /var/qmail2/bin/qmail-smtpd 2>&1
```

To what address the second `qmail-send` instance should listen depends very much on what its purpose is. If the purpose is to provide different connection policies (e.g. different DNS blacklists) for different domains, the server computer will need to manage multiple publicly accessible IP addresses, each with its own `tcpserver` and `qmail-smtpd`. The reason different connection policies cannot be implemented for different domains on a single shared IP address is that a connection policy, by definition, takes effect before data is sent. Thus, which domain's policy should be used is unknown until `qmail-smtpd` is run, which is too late.

Hiding Multiple Queues from the User

When a given computer has multiple qmail installations, it is sometimes desirable to hide the details of the different qmail queues from the users. For example, if a single computer is hosting several domains, each with different queue lifetimes, each mail that is sent must be fed to the correct queue, depending on which domain sent it. Most webmail applications will either use a single binary (usually `/usr/sbin/sendmail`) or a single address (usually 127.0.0.1, port 25) to send mail, regardless of which user is sending the mail. Unless this situation is handled specially, all mail sent from that webmail application will go through a single queue, rather than a different queue for each domain, and so they will all use the same queue settings (which invalidates the whole point of setting up separate queues in the first place).

There are multiple ways of handling this problem. A labor-intensive way is to install several versions of the webmail application, one for each domain. While conceptually simple, this quickly becomes an administrative nightmare, particularly when upgrading or reconfiguring the webmail software. A more transparent and maintainable technique is to create a wrapper script around the `qmail-queue` binary to deliver the message to the correct queue depending on its return address. As a simple example, imagine a computer responsible for both the 192.168.1.1 and 192.168.1.2 IP addresses. The 192.168.1.1 address is used for the `example.com` domain, and the 192.168.1.2 address is used for the `somewhere.net` domain. Each domain has its own queue—`example.com`'s queue is in `/var/qmail/queue` and `somewhere.net`'s queue is in `/var/qmail2/queue`—but the `/usr/sbin/sendmail` file (used by their shared webmail installation) can only be a symbolic link to one of them. In this case, it is a link to the `example.com` qmail installation's `sendmail` binary. To ensure that mail is delivered by the correct domain's qmail installation, a wrapper script around `example.com`'s `qmail-queue` binary can be used.

Here is a simple example:

```
#!/bin/bash
# Read envelope data (from file descriptor 1)
read -u 1 -d $'\0' sender
i=0
while read -u 1 -d $'\0' recipient ; do
    [ -z "$recipient" ] && break
    recipients[$i]="$recipient"
    i=$(($i+1))
done
# Build the envelope data back up
TMPFILE="$(mktemp -t qmailqueue.XXXXXXXXXXXXXXXXXX)"
printf '%s\0' "$sender" > "$TMPFILE"
for ((i=0;$i<${#recipients[*]};i=$i+1)) ; do
    printf '%s\0' "${recipients[$i]}" >> "$TMPFILE"
done
printf '\0' >> $tmpfile
# Extract the domain from the sender's address
FROMDOMAIN=${sender##*@}
# turn on case-insensitive matching
shopt -s -q nocasematch
# Invoke the domain-specific qmail-queue binary
case "$FROMDOMAIN" in
    example.com)
    /var/qmail/bin/qmail-queue-real 1<"$TMPFILE"
    exitvalue=$? ;;
*)
    /var/qmail2/bin/qmail-queue 1<"$TMPFILE"
    exitvalue=$? ;;
esac
# cleanup
rm $TMPFILE
exit $exitvalue
```

To use this script most transparently, one must first rename the real *qmail-queue* binary for the example.com domain from /var/qmail/bin/qmail-queue to /var/qmail/bin/qmail-queue-real. Then, save this script as /var/qmail/bin/ qmail-queue and make sure that it is both executable and readable. Thereafter, whenever mail is queued with example.com's *sendmail* binary, (or *qmail-smtpd*, *qmail-queue*, *qmail-inject*, *qmail-qmtpd*, or any other component that uses *qmail-queue*) this script will be invoked instead of the real *qmail-queue* binary. The script will make sure that the mail gets added to the queue corresponding to the sender's domain. The upside is that this works for any standard method of sending mail. Of course, the sender address this script relies upon can be forged (or mistyped) and may not reflect the domain of the actual sender.

In most cases, this is not a severe problem, but can expose the fact that there are multiple queues. The problem of message headers and envelope information potentially being forged is a difficult one. It is possible to be more thorough, and attempt making decisions about which queue to use based on other, more reliable information (such as the user name provided during SMTP-AUTH) but this is more involved and does not typically address every possible way of queueing mail. However, getting the mail into the right queue is only a problem when attempting to hide either the virtual nature of the server or the separation of its queues. By exposing the separation, such as by providing different IP addresses or port numbers to use for sending mail from each domain, the system's behavior becomes far more predictable. Not because the headers are restricted, but because which domain's queue is used becomes an explicit choice the user makes by submitting messages to a specific IP address or port number.

Virtualization is usually an attempt to share limited resources, such as servers, IP addresses, or system administrator's time. At some level, there is almost always a way to break the veil and discover the virtualization because some detail of the sharing is visible. In general, few people mind it, as long as mail gets where it needs to go.

Summary

This chapter has covered the set up of virtual domains and users within the qmail architecture, both how to use qmail's formidable virtualization features to achieve separate domain namespaces, and also how to further virtualize even the qmail queue itself to use different configuration settings. The next chapter will push the envelope of what the qmail architecture can do much further than virtualization. Filters around each architectural component, akin to the `qmail-queue` wrapper presented in this chapter, allow the administrator to radically change the system's behavior.

6
Filtering

It's been said before, and it's worth repeating: qmail is a very modular email architecture. Because of this modularity, it is relatively easy to alter the behavior of the overall system by wrapping the basic components or by inserting a script or program between them. Filtering email is a perfect example of the power of this design. This is done by filtering the communication between architectural components; so while filtering email is the primary operation discussed in this chapter, filtering architectural interfaces is the method by which this expansion or modification of the architecture is achieved.

Basic Filtering Architecture

The basic qmail architecture, trimmed down to just the parts relevant to delivery (and thus filtering) of email, is shown in the following figure:

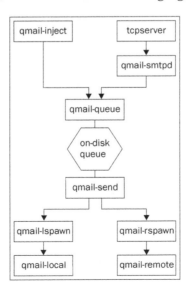

Almost any of qmail's components can be wrapped and used for filtering purposes. Which components to wrap depends on the specific behavior desired. In many cases there are multiple ways of achieving the same thing and choosing which method to use requires planning. For example, if some email needs to be blocked or rejected, it is better to catch that email earlier in its path through the system rather than later. This reduces the amount of time and resources spent on email that is not delivered. Thus, the most common place to block mail is before it is queued for delivery. Filtering mail (i.e. modifying it) is often done in multiple places, depending on what kind of filtering is desired. For example, filtering for spam is sometimes done before mail is queued, though this makes it harder to implement user-specific filtering rules completely. If user-specific filters are desired, filtering at the delivery stage is often preferable.

Exactly where a component is inserted affects what filtering options are available. For example, a wrapper around `qmail-queue` can examine the full content of an email, but does not know precisely where the email came from. A wrapper around `qmail-smtpd` knows exactly where the email originated, but in order to inspect the content of the email the wrapper must process SMTP itself, making the wrapper far more complicated and prone to security vulnerabilities. The following figure describes typical filters for each location in the architecture.

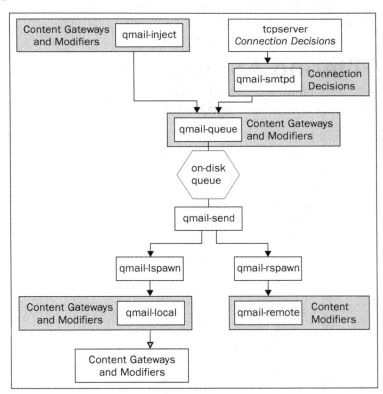

Connection decisions determine whether to allow a connection or not, and are based solely on information about the connection (such as the client's IP address and port number). A basic example of this is provided by the `tcprules` files discussed in Chapter 1. A **content gateway** is a filter that decides whether to allow a given email to continue to the next stage of delivery based on the content of that email. A **content modifier,** on the other hand, is a filter that always allows the email through to the next stage, but usually alters the email's content as it does so. In practice, the distinctions between these types of filters are often blurred, as some filters can both block and modify. Examples are given throughout the rest of this chapter.

The reasons for wrapping each component are relatively straightforward.

- `qmail-inject`: A wrapper around `qmail-inject` can make decisions about which users are allowed to send email, can prevent users from sending spam or viruses, can help fill out form-letter emails, or something similar.

- `qmail-smtpd`: A wrapper around `qmail-smtpd` can set useful environment variables (such as RELAYCLIENT), check for protocol conformance, or check the client against DNS blacklists, among other things.

- `qmail-queue`: A wrapper around `qmail-queue` can check messages for viruses, spam, valid DomainKeys signatures and similar tricks, and can even feed modified versions of the email to `qmail-queue` instead of the original.

- `qmail-remote`: A wrapper around `qmail-remote` is useful for making sure that all outbound email is properly signed with a DomainKeys signature or similar email modifications.

- `qmail-local`: A wrapper around `qmail-local` is similar in purpose to a `qmail-queue` wrapper. The difference is that by the time the message gets to this point in the delivery process, it is a copy of the message for a single recipient. This is a useful thing to know if different recipients have different filtering preferences. And, of course, `qmail-local` can deliver to programs like `procmail` and `maildrop` that both filter and discard mail according to recipient preferences.

In addition to wrapping each component, of course, the components themselves can be modified to perform a task, though this usually requires more programming experience. However, if speed is a consideration, modifying components is often faster than wrapping them.

The most commonly wrapped components are `qmail-queue` and `qmail-smtpd`, because the most common filters intercept spam and viruses. In addition to hand-written wrapper scripts, there are several popular `qmail-queue` wrappers available that provide an array of filtering options, including:

- Inter7's `simscan` (`http://www.inter7.com/?page=simscan`)
- Qscanq (`http://www.qscanq.org`)

- Bruce Guenter's *qmail-qfilter* (http://untroubled.org/qmail-qfilter)
- *qmail-scanner* (http://qmail-scanner.sourceforge.net)

These wrapper programs generally save incoming email to a file; feed it to other filtering or scanning programs (e.g. to detect viruses); and, depending on the result of these external programs, either delete, quarantine, or reject the email or feed it back to *qmail-queue* for delivery. They also can extract any MIME-encoded attachments from the email for separate scanning. Qscanq is the simplest of the three, supporting few virus scanners and no inherent spam scanning. It either silently destroys virus-laden email or rejects it. Inter7's simscan is more complex, supporting several virus scanners as well as the SpamAssassin's spamc scanner. simscan either rejects or destroys virus-infected messages and conditionally rejects, deletes, or passes-through messages based on their SpamAssassin score. The *qmail-scanner* wrapper is more complex, and because it is written in Perl rather than C, has more per-message overhead than the other wrappers. However, this wrapper supports almost all popular virus scanners, message quarantining, SpamAssassin analysis, internal pattern matching, and many other features. The most versatile wrapper is *qmail-qfilter*. It provides a mechanism to run arbitrary programs or scripts on each message and rejects, deletes, or passes through messages based on the result of each program.

The *qmail-smtpd* program is, unlike *qmail-queue*, more often wrapped with simple scripts and small, single-purpose programs instead of multi-purpose utility programs. As an example, included in the ucspi-tcp software package is a program called *rblsmtpd*. This program relies on the environment variable TCPREMOTEIP, as defined by *tcpserver*. It will look up that IP address in a DNS-based blacklist (specified on the command line) and, depending on whether the IP is listed in the blacklist or not, will either print an SMTP rejection message or execute the program specified in its arguments—usually, *qmail-smtpd*. For example, *rblsmtpd* can be used as follows:

```
tcpserver -u `id -u qmaild` -g `id -g qmaild` \
  0 smtp rblsmtpd -r some.blacklist.domain qmail-smtpd
```

In addition to wrappers, there are also several drop-in replacements for *qmail-smtpd*. For example, *mailfront* (http://untroubled.org/mailfront) by Bruce Guenter, supports SMTP-AUTH, virus scanning, sender/recipient filtering, and many other features. Linux Magic's *magic-smtpd* (http://www.linuxmagic.com/opensource/magicmail/magic-smtpd) is similar and includes features like SMTP tarpitting, user validation, TLS, SMTP-AUTH, and many others. These programs would be used as follows (using mailfront as an example):

```
tcpserver -u `id -u qmaild` -g `id -g qmaild` \
  0 smtp mailfront
```

The structure of these commands can be a bit confusing. The *tcpserver* program sets up the network connection and then runs a single program. *tcpserver*'s view of its arguments is that they are in four ordered categories:

tcpserver tcpserverArguments aProgramToRun argumentsToThatProgram

The way it identifies what program to run is, by simply assuming that the first argument that it doesn't understand (and doesn't start with a hyphen) is the name of a program and all subsequent text blocks are arguments to that program. For example, when using *rblsmtpd* with *qmail-smtpd*, *tcpserver* views it in the following manner:

tcpserver tcpserverArguments rblsmtpd argumentsToRblsmtpd

tcpserver knows nothing of *qmail-smtpd* or any other program; but because it cannot identify *rblsmtpd* it must therefore be the name of a program. Once the program runs, *tcpserver* has no further control over it. *rblsmtpd*, behaves similarly. When it runs, it views its arguments in four ordered categories:

rblsmtpd rblsmtpdArguments aProgramToRun argumentsToThatProgramIfAny

When it's used with *qmail-smtpd*, it sees this:

rblsmtpd rblsmtpdArguments *qmail-smtpd* argumentsToQmailSmtpdIfAny

Once *rblsmtpd* runs and makes its decision, it then executes whatever program the text *qmail-smtpd* identifies. Like *tcpserver*, when *rblsmtpd* runs a program, it has no control over it; unlike *tcpserver*, which spawns a child to run (exec) the program, *rblsmtpd* runs (execs) the named program itself, and the new program completely replaces *rblsmtpd* in memory.

This telescoping, cascading, or chaining behavior—where the wrapper does some action and then runs (execs) the next program in the chain—is a common wrapping technique.

Sending Mail Without a Queue

One of the nice things about having such a modular architecture is that pieces of the architecture can be rearranged or removed. A good example of doing this is removing the queue from the picture, so that messages are sent immediately to another email server. There are several ways of achieving this end depending on the specific behavior required. The two primary methods are described here.

Dr. Bernstein's website has simple directions (http://cr.yp.to/qmail/mini.html) for setting up a queue-less qmail installation that uses the **Quick Mail Queueing Protocol (QMQP)** to transmit email messages to another qmail server (or any server that understands QMQP). He calls this setup **mini-qmail**. QMQP (similar to QMTP) avoids some of the latency of SMTP, and optimizes message transmission. However, only qmail currently supports QMQP, and so it may not be the best option in a mixed environment. These instructions direct that the *qmail-queue* binary be replaced with the *qmail-qmqpc* binary. This program uses the same interface as *qmail-queue* but rather than queuing messages, it transmits them to another server via the QMQP protocol, as directed by the control/qmqpservers file (details are in the *qmail-qmqpc* man page).

Creating a queue-less qmail installation that uses SMTP is a little more work than the QMQP-only setup but it can cooperate with servers that do not support QMQP. The easiest way to do it is, similar to mini-qmail, to replace *qmail-queue* with a program that will instead transmit messages to a remote server. Such a program, akin to *qmail-qmqpc*, must support the *qmail-queue* interface. The *qmail-queue* replacement program does not, however, need to interact with the network; it can simply use *qmail-remote* to transmit messages via SMTP. For example, the following script could work:

```bash
#!/bin/bash
# read the envelope information first (from file descriptor 1)
read -u 1 -d $'\0' sender
i=0
while read -u 1 -d $'\0' recipient ; do
    [ -z "$recipient" ] && break
    recipients[$i]="$recipient"
    i=$(($i+1))
done
# Now, generate the Received header,
# feed the message to qmail-remote, and capture the output
printf 'Received: (qmail %i invoked by uid %i); %s\n%s\n' \
    "$$" "$UID" "$(date '+%d %b %Y %k:%M:%S %z')" "$(cat -)" | \
    /var/qmail/bin/qmail-remote \
    $SMARTHOST "$sender" "${recipients[@]}" | \
    while read -d $'\0' result ; do
        case "$result" in
            K*) # success
            exit 0;;
            Z*) # temporary failure
            exit 71;;
            D*) # permanent failure
            exit 31;;
        esac
    done
```

For this script to work, the SMARTHOST environment variable must be defined or $SMARTHOST must be replaced by the correct host (either a hostname or a square bracketed IP address) to send mails to.

Blocking Viruses

The most common means of transferring viruses to new vulnerable computers is through email. Originally, viruses preferred to invisibly infect innocuous files that were later transferred from computer to computer at the behest of a person sharing files for legitimate purposes. While this can still happen, the overwhelming majority of virus-laden email is sent by autonomous viruses that either have randomly generated recipients or have found recipient addresses on the infected computer. More to the point, these emails generally contain nothing of value. With that change in behavior, the best way to handle emails containing viruses has also changed. In the past, the expectation was that email containing a virus should be modified, the virus stripped out, and the sanitized message delivered to its original destination. These days, infected emails are so rarely legitimate that rather than delivering them, the most common response is simply to delete the infected messages entirely.

Both policies, however, rely upon detecting infected emails, for which there are many options.

Heavyweight Filtering

Heavyweight filtering is the filtering that most often comes to mind for virus eradication. Each email is decoded, attachments if any are separated, and all of the component parts of the email are scanned with virus scanning software to determine if they contain a virus. Such scanning is considered heavyweight because of the sheer enormity of the task. Virus scanners maintain large databases of every known computer virus and how to detect it. There are millions of different species of computer viruses, and new viruses are discovered almost hourly. A good virus scanning installation must maintain this large database, test for every single virus in that database, and also keep this database updated. Usually these tasks are automated, but this scanning method is time-consuming for every message. In high-load situations, such virus detection might not be feasible.

Some of the most common virus scanners are:

- AVG Anti-Virus
- Trend InterScan VirusWall
- F-Prot Antivirus scanner
- NAI/McAfee scanner

- H+BEDV's AntiVir scanner
- Kaspersky's AVPLinux scanner
- Command's virus scanner
- the F-Secure Anti-Virus scanner
- the InocuLAN Anti-Virus scanner
- BitDefender Linux Edition
- Central Command's Vexira anti-virus scanner
- the ESET NOD32 Anti-Virus scanner
- the open-source Clam Anti-Virus (ClamAV) scanner

These scanners must be *hooked into* the qmail architecture to scan each email. The most common way of doing this is with a wrapper around `qmail-queue`. Some virus scanners come with a `qmail-queue` wrapper; however, most require a separate wrapper, such as those discussed previously.

Lightweight Filtering

There are other options for protecting email users from viruses that do not require a heavyweight approach or can reduce the load on a heavyweight virus scanner. The simplest options start with policy decisions, such as banning certain types of files. For example, most viruses are Microsoft Windows executable files—a fact that has made banning executable files from email a popular policy. Simple filters that reject email containing attachments whose names end in `.exe` (filters such as `qmail-scanner`) can be effective, however, not all Microsoft Windows executable file names end in `.exe`. Indeed, they can actually use almost any suffix and still be recognized as executable by Windows. However, all Microsoft Windows executable files begin with information that tells Windows how to load the program. This information is the same in all Windows programs and is required in order to run the file. It is small, always at the beginning of the file, and thus easily detected. There is a small patch for `qmail-smtpd`, written by Russ Nelson (http://www.qmail.org/ qmail-smtpd-viruscan-1.3.patch) that makes it easy to enforce a policy banning Windows executable files from email. This patch requires very little overhead and is effective even in high-load situations. To hide from such filters, some viruses send themselves as zip-compressed archives and rely on the recipient to uncompress the virus and run it. ZIP files, like executable files, all begin with a similar pattern and can be identified and banned with Russ Nelson's patch. Be warned, however, that some file formats—such as some OpenOffice files—are, unbeknownst to the user, really zip-compressed collections of several components, and banning all ZIP files also bans these files.

Not all viruses are executable files so Russ Nelson's patch is not a complete solution. For example, scripts (like Visual Basic .vbs files) and Microsoft Office macro-viruses are not technically executable files, and so cannot be blocked by this patch. Additionally, it might not be feasible to ban executable files and/or ZIP files from email. However, when such measures are possible, simple filters such as Russ Nelson's patch or a suffix-detector provide an effective first line of defense against viruses.

Stopping Spam from Getting In

Eliminating spam is one of the most important tasks of today's email administrators. There are two equally important facets to eliminating spam: preventing it from being sent by your server and preventing it from being delivered to your users. Of the two, preventing it from being delivered is often the hardest.

Sender Validation

Strictly speaking, sender validation is not an anti-spam technique, though it is often regarded as such. One of the interesting details of the SMTP protocol is that the sender of a given message is not restricted to the address of the actual sender. A person sending a message can specify any return address, just as they can specify any destination address. In a trustworthy environment, where no one has a reason to hide his or her identity, this is not a problem. However, on today's networks, viruses, scammers, spammers, and so-called phishers all wish to hide their identity when sending email.

The reason sender validation is usually considered an anti-spam technique is the belief that if spammers could not hide their identity, spam would be easier to block. However, it is important to recognize that a spammer can send spam that correctly identifies himself or herself as the sender. Accurate sender addresses do not make the mail any less spammy, but makes messages from known spammers easy to refuse and messages from known non-spammers impossible to mistake for spam. Unfortunately, qmail-compatible software for blocking specific validated senders does not exist.

There have been many ideas for reliably verifying email senders. The two most popular are the **Sender Policy Framework (SPF)** and DomainKeys. DomainKeys is an earlier version of **DomainKey Identified Mail (DKIM)**, which is not as widely deployed or supported as DomainKeys. However, given that it will shortly (as of this writing) be approved by the IETF, DKIM will eventually be widely implemented.

SPF

The basic idea behind SPF is that a domain should specify (in DNS) precisely which servers are authorized to send its email. Thus, an email claiming to be from a particular domain (such as ebay.com) but not originating from one of that domain's approved servers is considered a forgery. This works well in most circumstances, but its drawback is it breaks a widely used feature of email called forwarding, and not just for SPF users, but for anyone contacting an SPF-using domain.

People often have email addresses that are merely forwarding addresses such that all mail sent to that address is resent to another address. On virtually every email server prior to the invention of SPF, forwarded email was delivered unmodified. The problem with this approach has been illustrated with the help of the following figure:

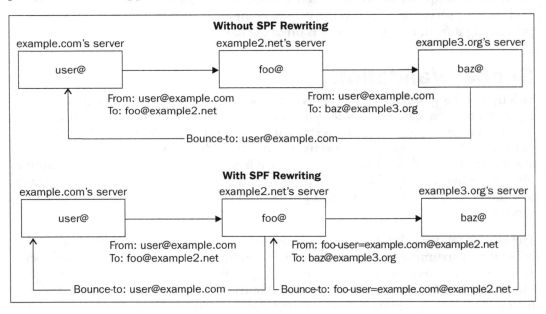

Imagine that the address foo@example2.net is a forwarding address that forwards to baz@example3.org. If a message is sent from user@example.com to foo@example2.net, the example2.net server then sends the message to the example3.org server. From the example3.org server's perspective, the example2.net server is sending email claiming to be from example.com. If example.com happens to publish an SPF record asserting that its email only originates from its own servers (which it did), and if example3.org blocks messages based on SPF information, it will refuse the user@example.com message forwarded by the example2.net server. This thwarts a viable (and popular) method of managing email accounts. The SPF workaround is to re-encode email return addresses so that each server only sends from its own domain. For example, `example2.net` could re-encode the return address to look like `foo-user=example.com@example2.net`, so the message does not appear to be claiming to be from `example.com`. If the message bounced back from `example3.org` for some reason, `example2.net` would receive it and could then decode the return address and bounce it back to the original sender, `user@example.com`. The problem with this solution is that a spammer could convince the `example2.net` server to relay spam by sending spam to `foo-anyuser=anydomain.com@example2.net` or a similar address. To prevent such abuse, each server will need to remember every email it forwarded for every user, so that it can refuse to relay bounces (or spam that looks like a bounce) that are for messages it didn't send. To be more to the point, each server will have to remember all of these messages until it can be certain that these emails will not bounce, which is an unpredictable amount of time. For example, the `example2.net` server cannot know whether the `example3.org` server is the message's final stop or whether it will be forwarded again and then bounce—keep in mind that a message can sit in a server's queue for a long time (typically up to seven days) before it is bounced.

DomainKeys

The DomainKeys concept is to cryptographically sign all messages with a public key encryption system, where the signature asserts that a server approved by the domain has sent the email. The information necessary to verify the validity of the signature is published in DNS, so that any server may validate the signature and prove that the message was signed by a server approved by that domain to send email. Thus, for a domain that asserts (in a DomainKeys policy record stored in DNS) that it signs all of its email, a message missing a signature or containing an incorrect signature is considered a forgery. Unlike SPF, this allows emails to be forwarded without being modified. The caveat is that DomainKeys requires that messages not be modified (between the DomainKeys signature and the end of the message). Thus, while Received headers and any other headers prepended to the message are acceptable, other modifications—such as spam-filter headers or signatures appended to either the end of the message or the end of the headers—can invalidate the DomainKeys signature. The DomainKeys specification includes the ability to name, in the signature (in an *h=* tag), what headers were originally included in the signature. This makes the signature much more tolerant of header modification, as additional headers (such as spam-filter headers) inserted in the wrong place in the message can be excluded from the signature. However, the body of the message and the headers that were included in the signature cannot change without invalidating the signature.

Russ Nelson has contributed significantly to qmail's ability to verify and sign messages with DomainKeys. Most significantly, he is the original author of the libdomainkeys library (`http://domainkeys.sourceforge.net`), which provides many ways of creating and validating DomainKeys signatures.

Russ Nelson also wrote a patch to the qmail source that creates a new component, *qmail-dk* (http://www.qmail.org/qmail-1.03-dk-0.53.patch), that can be used as a wrapper around *qmail-queue* for signing and verifying DomainKeys signatures. This program is convenient, but not always necessary. The libdomainkeys package includes a utility called *dktest* that can, with the appropriate shell-script glue, provide some of the basic features that *qmail-dk* provides. For example, to verify DomainKeys signatures in incoming email and add a header proclaiming the result, a script like the following will work:

```
#!/bin/sh
[ "$DKQUEUE" ] || DKQUEUE=/var/qmail/bin/qmail-queue
if printenv | grep -q '^DKVERIFY=' ; then
  tmp=`mktemp -t dk.verify.XXXXXXXXXXX`
  cat - >"$tmp"
  (dktest -v <"$tmp" 2>/dev/null | awk 'NR>1' ; \
    cat "$tmp" ) | "$DKQUEUE"
  retval=$?
  rm "$tmp"
  exit $retval
else
  exec "$DKQUEUE"
fi
```

This script can, in conjunction with the QMAILQUEUE patch (or as a *qmail-queue* replacement, provided that the real *qmail-queue* can still be used with a different name) tag each incoming email with a "DomainKey-Status" header, recording the results of checking the DomainKeys signature. The DKQUEUE environment variable is consulted for the location of the *qmail-queue* binary, and the DKVERIFY environment variable is used to enable verification.

The *qmail-dk* program serves two purposes: it verifies signatures (like the above script), and it creates signatures. Because *qmail-dk* is a *qmail-queue* wrapper, it must decide whether to sign a message when the message is queued. In order to sign all messages, every part of the system that queues messages must use it—from *qmail-smtpd* to *qmail-inject* to *qmail-local* (which queues messages in response to delivery instructions). Unfortunately, *qmail-dk* does not support the inclusion of an *h=* tag in the signature.

An alternative to wrapping *qmail-queue* with something like *qmail-dk* is to wrap *qmail-remote*. This signs all remotely delivered messages, no matter how they were enqueued. While *qmail-dk* does not serve easily as a *qmail-remote* wrapper, the following script (using *dktest*) is a suitable option.

This script, which supports the `h=` tag, presumes that its name is *qmail-remote* and that the original *qmail-remote* was renamed *qmail-remote.orig*:

```
#!/bin/bash
[ "$DKSIGN" ] || DKSIGN="/etc/domainkeys/%/default"
[ "$DKREMOTE" ] || DKREMOTE=/var/qmail/bin/qmail-remote.orig
if [[ $DKSIGN == *%* ]] ; then
  DOMAIN="${DOMAIN:-${2##*@}}"
  DKSIGN="${DKSIGN%%*}${DOMAIN}${DKSIGN#*%}"
fi
if [ -f "$DKSIGN" ] ; then
  tmp=$( mktemp -t dk.sign.XXXXXXXXXX )
  cat - >"$tmp"
  (dktest -s "$DKSIGN" -c nofws -h <"$tmp" 2>/dev/null | \
    sed 's/; d=.*;/; d='"$DOMAIN"';/'; \
    cat "$tmp" ) | \
    "$DKREMOTE" "$@"
  retval=$?
  rm "$tmp"
  exit $retval
else
  exec "$DKREMOTE" "$@"
fi
```

With this script, the environment variable DKSIGN specifies the location of the private key for the signing process, DKREMOTE specifies the location of the original *qmail-remote* program, and finally, DOMAIN specifies the sending domain (if it is unspecified, the script will assume the domain is the sender's domain). More conveniently, just like *qmail-dk*, DKSIGN can contain a percent sign (%) that is replaced by the signing domain name, thus making signing for multiple domains with separate keys more convenient.

Identifying Spam

Identifying spam is a complex task relying on one fundamental assumption: spam is not normal email and is not sent in the normal way. Now, at one level, this assumption seems obvious: of course spam is abnormal, and of course spam is sent by bulk mailers or virus bots or other unusual software. Nearly all of the effective anti-spam tactics rely on one or both of these details. For that reason, the distinction between real email (or ham) and spam email is precisely what spammers attempt to blur. Once spam is identified, it can either be tagged or blocked.

Lightweight

Lightweight methods for identifying spam are considered lightweight because they do not rely on complex analysis of email in order to make decisions, and the decisions are almost always binary: each email is accepted or rejected, with no gray area in between. How this decision is reached generally depends on how much information is available when the decision is made. In some cases, email is considered spam before the sender has sent even a single character of the email. If it is blocked at that point, bandwidth is not wasted in receiving the message. The methods described here are not an exhaustive list, but merely a set of popular examples.

Domain Name System Black-Lists

The technology known as **Domain Name System Black-List (DNSBL)** is a method for quickly deciding which messages are not acceptable. Essentially, the idea is this: spammers have a limited number of computers, and once these are identified, no messages from them need to be accepted. This of course makes the underlying assumption that messages from spammer-owned computers are always spam, and messages from other computers are never spam. The lists of computers known or suspected to be under spammer control are stored in a public database (namely, the DNS database). When a computer attempts to contact an email server using a DNSBL, it is checked on in the public database. If the connecting computer is listed as a spammer, the attempt is rejected.

Unfortunately, these public databases are far from perfect — some people who are listed are not spammers, and many spammers are not listed at all. As a result, DNSBLs are rather blunt instruments, to be used with care. Because of the proliferation of spam, however, many feel that the use of such blacklists is absolutely essential. Before using a blacklist, however, make sure that its policies regarding what senders get listed make sense for your server.

Checking for SMTP Violations

Another technique for quickly identifying spam is to categorize a given computer as a spammer based on its disregard for SMTP protocol details. For example, SMTP clients are required to wait until the server greets them to begin sending data. Spammers, however, are frequently in a hurry, and most servers do not object to receiving incoming email all at once. For this reason, spammers often begin transmitting data as quickly as possible without waiting for the server's participation. It is easy for a server to wait a second before greeting the client, just to see if the client will wait to be greeted. Not waiting for a greeting is an easily detected violation of the SMTP protocol common to many spammers.

Spammers often attempt to gain anonymity by sending email through someone else's computer, often exploiting unusual software in the process. For example, unsecured HTTP proxies can hide the spammer's identity, but send HTTP commands in addition to SMTP commands. In order for such subterfuge to work, the spammer relies on most servers ignoring the HTTP commands and accepting the SMTP commands. However, the presence of both types of commands is an easy way to identify a sender who is doing something improper and, therefore, is a spammer.

The popular greylisting technique also fits into this spammer-identifying category. Greylisting is a technique of validating sending clients by temporarily refusing to accept messages from unrecognized clients. Once an initial attempt is made and fails with a temporary error code, that sender is added to the list of recognized senders. Further delivery attempts are accepted. When this happens to a typical email, the sending server waits and re-attempts delivery later. Spammers, however, often do not care whether their messages are delivered and do not re-attempt later, identifying themselves as spammers. This technique can be altered to require specific messages to be retried rather than specific clients, but the fundamental concept is the same.

Monitoring protocol violations, however, is obviously not a full solution; spammers only need to use software that fully implements SMTP and they will get through. The reason this is still a successful method of detecting spammers is that spammers find it inconvenient to obey all of the SMTP requirements, and most recipient servers are not picky about protocol violations.

Pattern Matching

Once a message is transmitted, heavyweight scanners can analyze it in depth. Looking for simple patterns in an email's text is often surprisingly effective. For example, emails naming obscure pharmaceuticals or beginning with the phrase "Dear friend", or those obfuscating English words with misspellings and numbers (for example, "pr0n") are often spam. On the other hand, these patterns are also in messages that discuss spam, and can mistakenly identify a message as spam when it is not.

Heavyweight

While lightweight spam identification techniques are often effective, their simplicity leaves them vulnerable to avoidance or compensation techniques implemented by spammers. Heavyweight spam identification, on the other hand, is designed to be more robust and to adapt as spammers change their tactics.

Bayesian and other Machine-Learning Techniques

A relatively recent development in spam fighting has been the popularization of Bayesian networks to identify spam, beginning in 2002 (first proposed in 1998). Bayesian networks work in terms of probability: each word or phrase in a message has a certain probability of identifying the message as spam. The more "probably spam" words in a message, the more likely the message is spam. Similarly, the more "probably not spam" words in a message; the less likely the message is spam. What makes this technique particularly interesting is its ability to use email examples provided by the user to discover important words and phrases and to fine-tune its identifying power (probability) over time. In this way, the filter learns what spam looks like and adapts as spam changes. Messages from family members, for example, can be analyzed by the Bayesian classifier to discover what specific names, words, and/or phrases are less likely to be used in spam, and what rarely used words or nonsensical word pairs are more likely to be used in spam. There are many examples of scanners that work this way, including:

- SpamProbe (http://spamprobe.sourceforge.net)
- SpamBayes (http://spambayes.sourceforge.net)
- Bogofilter (http://bogofilter.sourceforge.net)

Bayesian classification is a simple method of machine learning, and is susceptible to obfuscation of the content of the email. However, the idea of applying machine-learning techniques to the problem of spam identification is a powerful one. Several software projects are available that use more advanced mathematical models than the basic Bayesian model. For example, the CRM114 (http://crm114.sourceforge.net/) filter organizes words and phrases into hidden Markov models rather than Bayesian networks, and the DSPAM (http://dspam.nuclearelephant.com/) software adds neural networks and several advanced enhancements to standard Bayesian learning and classification techniques.

Ensemble Identification

One of the most popular forms of heavyweight analysis is the ensemble analysis; also referred to as the toolkit or arsenal approach. Rather than analyzing messages using a particular method, messages are examined with multiple methods, and the outputs of these methods are considered recommendations rather than authoritative decisions. These recommendations are combined with a weighted scoring system that allows techniques with low effectiveness to be taken into consideration. Messages with scores over a certain threshold are then considered spam, while messages under that threshold are not. One of the most popular examples of this type of spam identification technique is SpamAssassin (http://spamassassin.apache.org/).

SpamAssassin uses a large library of pattern-based filters, consults DNSBLs and several online spam databases, and also includes a Bayesian analyzer. The benefit of this approach is that new ideas in identifying spam can be added to the arsenal as they are developed. The catch, however, is that the software is very complicated, and has more overhead than simpler or more straightforward classification techniques because it uses all of the identification techniques rather than just one of them. Additionally, the expected level of accuracy must weigh the influence of the techniques used. Getting the right balance between rules is difficult to gauge in the general case. SpamAssassin, for example, carefully tailors the relative weights of rules in its collection to be accurate over a large set of unrelated emails.

Quarantines and Challenges

Perhaps the most involved filters are the kind that hold email messages hostage while a human decides whether they are spam (and should be deleted) or are ham (and should be delivered). These types of filters fall into two categories: quarantines and challenges. With a quarantine the recipient decides whether a message is spam or not, while with a challenge, the sender must certify a message is not spam. The more common of the two is quarantine, usually combined with heavyweight scoring. Because heavyweight identification typically places email somewhere on a continuum between spam and ham, messages not considered ham are often delivered to a special folder for holding spam. This folder is a quarantine where messages are examined by the recipient, and mistaken categorizations can be identified.

Challenge-based spam identification is less popular, but also effective. One of the most popular forms of challenge-based spam identification is called **Tagged Message Delivery Agent (TMDA)**. When a message is received, it is stored in a holding area while a challenge message is sent back to the sender. The challenge message contains instructions to be followed by the sender so as to identify himself or herself as a non-spammer, such as visiting a message-specific URL or replying to a message-specific email address. When the sender's validating action is performed, the original message is delivered, and in some cases the sender is then added to a list of known good senders so that no challenges are made in the future. This technique is effective against spam, because it requires a valid return address in addition to some of the spammer's precious time. On a usual spammer scale, where millions of messages are sent in an average hour, responding to the TMDA message is not worth the effort. On the other hand, TMDA challenges are frequently effective against ordinary busy people as well. Some people consider challenges to prove that they are not spammers rude or, at the very least, a waste of time. Consider, for example, a person asking an expert a question. The expert might wish to respond, but balk at spending time verifying his non-spammer status. Of course, such situations are easily avoided through judicious use of white lists, but TMDA and other challenge-based methods make such problems easy to overlook.

Mistakes

One of the most critical things to consider when evaluating any anti-spam technique is the problem of mistakes. No technique is perfect, and the questions to answer when evaluating a technique include:

1. Can false positives (incorrectly tagged or blocked email) be detected?
2. Can false positives be fixed?
3. Can false negatives (spam that was not blocked or tagged) be corrected?
4. Can user errors be fixed?

In the lightweight categories, detecting false positives is problematic because messages identified as spam are often prevented from being delivered. For example, if a domain is mistakenly listed in a DNSBL, all email communication with that domain is cut off, making it difficult for users of that domain to complain that their messages are not being delivered. Often, the only way for domains using the DNSBL to discover the error is for someone from the blocked domain to inform their intended recipient of the problem via a non-email method. This is, of course, only possible if all affected parties have both the desire and ability to use a non-email method of contact. Rather than blocking email that is considered spam, the alternative is to tag it with an identifying header. Email so tagged is delivered to a special spam folder, quarantine area, or something similar. This allows spam-like email to be reviewed for mistakes, but does not take advantage of the primary purpose of lightweight filters: to make quick, final decisions and avoid spending time and resources analyzing each email in depth. Thus tagging email only makes sense when using a heavyweight filter.

Whether mistakes can be fixed is another issue. With learning filters, such as Bayesian classifiers, correcting mistakes and thus improving accuracy is fundamental to the filter's design. On the other hand, informing the filter of its mistakes is frequently inconvenient, particularly with a large group of users who use different mail clients. Some filters, like DSPAM, provide a full web interface for submitting incorrectly tagged email messages, while others rely on command-line access to the mail server or some concoction by the system administrator. A good way to handle such tools in an IMAP-based environment is by creating magic folders that will — either by some server-based hook, `cron`, or some other method — cause the spam identification system to re-interpret messages placed in them.

On the other hand, correcting errors in a DNSBL or a spam database ranges anywhere from impossible to difficult, depending on the philosophy of those who maintain it. It is often necessary to use a local hand-written white list to avoid or countermand known misidentifications in such lightweight spam prevention techniques.

Stopping Spam from Getting Out

Preventing users from receiving spam is only half of the spam battle. The other half is to avoid sending spam. This may seem like a simple task on a user-by-user basis, but preventing users and your email system from sending spam on a wide-scale basis is more difficult. How to accomplish this depends upon the environment (i.e. how users send email), the resources devoted to the task, and the level of trust and convenience afforded to each user.

An obvious way to address to the problem is to treat outbound email similarly to inbound email. For example, software such as SpamAssassin can scan each email before it is sent, and prevent messages identified as spam from being sent. This, however, is frequently overkill, and is particularly unnecessary if one's users are unlikely to be spammers.

Sender Restrictions

A simplistic approach is to perform basic checks on outbound email, such as ensuring the sender of every email is a valid recipient, limiting the amount of email a sender sends per hour, prohibiting the use of BCC: headers, or something similar. These restrictions, of course, can be onerous, depending on the users being supported, so limits should be chosen carefully.

Bounce-Back Spam

Qmail is often criticized for its default policy of accepting all email destined for domains it considers local and then generating bounce messages for any email whose recipient does not exist. While this is a legitimate practice according to the SMTP protocol, it creates the problem of bounce-back spam (also known as blow-back or back-scatter). The problem stems from the fact that the sender's address might be inaccurate or invalid. When a spammer sends several million messages to random usernames at one of the configured local domains, qmail accepts them all and then generates bounces for all of the non-existent addresses (likely, all of them). Since the sender's address for these emails is probably inaccurate, either qmail is left with a large number of undeliverable bounce messages in its queue or qmail sends bounce messages to whatever legitimate email addresses the spammer chose to use as the return addresses. For example, a spammer can send a message with a return address of you@yourdomain.com to lasdkfkjhqw@example.com. The *lasdkfkjhqw* user likely does not exist at example.com, and if example.com is using an unmodified qmail installation, it will send a bounce message to you@yourdomain.com to inform you that the spammer's message could not be delivered.

Recipient Validation

A partial solution to the problem of bounce-back spam is to modify qmail so that it will only accept messages addressed to valid recipients. For example, a modified (or wrapped) qmail can check whether a given user exists in the recipient domain rather than simply checking whether the recipient domain is listed in the `control/rcpthosts` file. Checking whether a user exists can be a complicated task. For example, mailing lists often use temporary addresses for administrative tasks (like handling user subscription requests) and virtual domains can have external user databases that qmail cannot access easily (such as vpopmail or GNU Mailman domains). As such, there are many different patches to qmail that use different methods of determining whether a user exists or not. Some of the most popular are:

- Oliver Neubauer's validrcptto patch (`http://www3.sympatico.ca/humungusfungus/code/validrcptto.html`) considers a user valid if it is listed in the file `control/validrcptto`. This introduces two complications: first, the user list must be kept up to date, and second, no wild-card addresses are allowed (such as those used by many mailing list software packages, like ezmlm and GNU Mailman).

- Dr. Erwin Hoffmann wrote, as part of his SPAMCONTROL collection of patches, the RECIPIENTS extension patch (`http://www.fehcom.de/qmail/recipients/recipients-044_tgz.bin`). This is similar to the validrcptto patch, but relies on a CDB file rather than a text file to list all the valid recipients (making lookups faster, particularly when the list of valid recipients is long). It also accepts all wildcard extension addresses of the addresses listed in its CDB file. In other words, if the address `you@example.com` is listed, it accepts `you-anything@example.com` as well. Like the validrcptto patch, the centralized list of users must be kept up to date.

- Paul Jarc wrote the realrcptto patch (`http://multivac.cwru.edu/qmail/`) to use the same tests that *qmail-send* uses to choose a delivery location. This works well when users are defined entirely within qmail's configuration files, or when all delivery locations are accessible by the *qmaild* user (i.e. the user that runs *qmail-smtpd*) but does not work well otherwise. For example, this patch accepts all messages for virtual domains controlled entirely by a single `.qmail-default` file (such as vpopmail domains and GNU Mailman domains) and does not correctly reject messages addressed to recipients that do not exist for those domains (because *qmail-send* would not reject those messages either; the bounce message normally comes from the vpopmail or Mailman software).

- Jay Soffian's RCPTCHECK patch (http://www.soffian.org/downloads/qmail/qmail-smtpd-doc.html) relies on a sysadmin-provided external script or program to determine whether a recipient is acceptable or not. In a sense, this is the most flexible approach. It can be made to use any method necessary to validate a user, and allows the script to run as whatever user is necessary to perform the verification without requiring *qmail-smtpd* to have sufficient privileges to do so itself. However, this flexibility requires the sysadmin to write the script or program to perform the validation, which is more work.

This task does not absolutely require patching qmail; a *qmail-queue* wrapper can also perform it. Using a wrapper rather than a patch in this case has the drawback that the entire message must be received before the *qmail-queue* wrapper is triggered. A patch can check the recipients' validity as the sender lists them. If the recipients are invalid, rejecting them earlier saves bandwidth.

None of these methods is a full solution to the problem of bounce-back spam, because none of them can guarantee that a given message is deliverable.

Recipient Validation is Insufficient

User validation is sufficient to prevent bounces in many cases, but some common examples where bounce-back spam cannot be prevented include:

- **The recipient does not have enough room in his or her mailbox to deliver the message.** Normally, qmail simply leaves such messages in its queue and keeps retrying delivery until the message is either delivered or it is older than the allowable queue lifetime (defined in control/queuelifetime), normally seven days.

- **The recipient forwards the message elsewhere.** If the user's email is forwarded to a non-local account, it might not be deliverable right away, for a variety of reasons that depend on the destination server — the destination might be offline, might have temporary problems, the user might have run out of quota on that system, or any of a number of other problems may occur.

- **The recipient refuses the message in his or her** .qmail **file.** If the user's .qmail file contains something like: |bouncesaying 'go away', then incoming messages are bounced to their return address.

- **The recipient set a vacation message.** If the user's .qmail file contains something like: |autorespond 'I am on vacation.', then a message is sent to the return address of any message sent to that user.

- **The recipient may be a mailing list**. Messages to mailing lists often generate automated response emails, such as warnings that only subscribers can post or instructions for how to subscribe to the list. Generally accepted best practice for mailing lists allowing anyone to self-subscribe is to require address confirmation. In other words, when someone attempts to subscribe, the list sends a message to the subscribing address with instructions for completing the subscription (this prevents people from subscribing others to lists without their knowledge). Thus, if a spammer sends a message to a mailing list's subscription address, a confirmation email is sent to the return address of the spammer's email.

Though bounce-back spam can never be fully eliminated, validating recipients still dramatically reduces the problem.

One of the downsides of validating recipients, however, is it allows spammers to quickly discover (via the guess-and-check method) what users are valid on such a system, and in future the spammer can direct spam to only those recipients. While this is technically possible, in practice, it is uncommon that spammers spend the time necessary to track the success of each address, because obtaining valid addresses to spam can be achieved with much less time-consuming methods.

Summary

This chapter covered the general topic of expanding the qmail architecture, with particular focus on the details of spam and virus prevention. Many different techniques for addressing the many facets of spam and viruses in today's world were discussed. Armed with this knowledge, a system administrator can harden an email system against spam in ways that are effective, efficient, and appropriate for a system's particular needs, limitations, and available resources. The next chapter covers more advanced topics—SSL support and mailing list support—that rely in different ways upon the understanding of the architecture presented in this chapter.

7
Advanced Features

The foundation of knowledge presented so far in this book is enough to provide some intuition about how to get started with implementing most desired email server features. To provide some examples for building upon this foundation, this chapter explores SSL encryption (also known as TLS) and efficient mailing list implementations. There is, of course, a nearly unlimited set of further topics and features that could be discussed, but these two are a good start.

SSL Encryption

The Internet is extremely powerful and flexible because of the way it works, although people are frequently surprised by how it works. When information (like a bit of text, a picture, or an email) is sent across the network, the sending computer puts the information into a packet, or series of packets, and hands them to a computer closer to the destination computer. In the end, this process resembles taking a postcard and handing it to someone else to be delivered. The person receiving the postcard looks at the address and hands it to someone else who is a little bit closer to the addressee. Computer networks are somewhat more formal and have a better sense (usually) of who the next-closest computer is, but the process is essentially the same. It is common for seventeen or so computers to handle a packet before it reaches its destination. The text of the postcard, or content of the packet, is available for anyone to read, if they so choose. Most computers do not examine the contents of the packets they relay, because they have other things to do, but there is nothing preventing them from doing so.

The entire scope of email content transmitted over the Internet this way—everything from stock tips to love letters to bank passwords—is exposed to unauthorized interception as it crosses networks, from machine to machine. In other words, things not everyone should read are transmitted in a way that anyone in the middle is able to intercept. In the case of regular mail, the solution is to forgo the use of postcards for anything private and instead write a letter secured in an envelope. In the world of computers, the solution is to use encryption.

There are many forms of encryption available for different purposes, but the basic concept is common to all of them: encryption is designed to guarantee only those who should read something can read it. For email, there are many ways to use encryption. When discussing email servers, encryption usually involves encrypting communication between SMTP servers using **Secure Sockets Layer (SSL)** encryption or **Transport Layer Security (TLS)** encryption. The SSL acronym is a reference to network connections in UNIX, which are called sockets. The difference between SSL and TLS is somewhat blurry because they both use the same encryption technology and are occasionally used interchangeably. To be more precise, however, the two terms are used to distinguish between encryption that starts at the same time as the network connection (SSL) and encryption that begins after the connection is established (TLS). Because the encryption must begin as the network connection is established, SSL encryption generally requires a distinct network port but does not change the underlying communication protocol. For example, SMTPS (the SSL version of SMTP) uses port 465 rather than the SMTP-standard port 25. TLS encryption, on the other hand, is an extension to the protocol implemented in a backwards-compatible way. In the case of SMTP, TLS encryption adds a single command, STARTTLS, to the protocol that directs the server to begin encrypting the network conversation. As such, it can be added to an SMTP server without requiring the server's clients to be aware of the change.

Qmail does not support SSL or TLS by default but this feature can be added to qmail in several ways, depending on when and where encryption is used. There are two primary opportunities for using encryption: when receiving email and when sending email. As is usually the case with the qmail architecture, there are two ways of implementing encryption: with a patch and with a wrapper.

Patch vs. Wrapper

The difference between using a patch and using a wrapper is based on their fundamental design difference: one *modifies* qmail (a patch), one *uses* qmail (a wrapper). Because a wrapper is a separate program, it creates an additional need for communication between different programs on the server: the wrapper and the qmail component it wraps. This leads to an increased overhead and latency. On the other hand, using a wrapper does not require modification to qmail itself, so it is less likely to cause security problems and can be easily removed if there is a problem with it.

The primary SSL/TLS patch was written by Frederick Vermeulen (http://inoa.net/qmail-tls/). There are several options for providing SSL service by means of a wrapper, but the most popular include André Oppermann's patch to *tcpserver* (http://www.nrg4u.com/), and stunnel (http://www.stunnel.org/). Another valid option, of course, is to replace *qmail-smtpd* with a program that understands SSL and TLS itself, such as Bruce Guenter's mailfront (http://untroubled.org/mailfront/).

When Receiving Email

The reasons to use encryption when receiving email are numerous. The standard reason is for privacy—i.e. keeping the content of email away from prying eyes. However, another common reason for needing the security and cryptographic privacy that encryption affords is SMTP-AUTH. When submitting email via SMTP and using the SMTP-AUTH extension to authorize the submission, usually both a username and password are sent over the network to the mail server. This information makes protecting this communication from interception especially important.

The most basic operational difference between handling the encryption within `qmail-smtpd` (i.e. with Vermeulen's patch or a replacement like `mailfront`) and handling the encryption in a wrapper around `qmail-smtpd` (i.e. Oppermann's patch or `stunnel`) is that changing the SMTP server makes it easier to support TLS (as it is an extension to the SMTP protocol). Oppermann's patch, for example, only supports SMTPS, (SSL encryption) not the STARTTLS extension to the SMTP protocol. `stunnel` can support the STARTTLS extension, but currently this requires patching the `stunnel` source code.

When evaluating the options, it is important to consider the security ramifications of the choice. Bruce Guenter's `mailfront` is a powerful tool (see Chapters 2 and 6); it is essentially a replacement for `qmail-smtpd` that adds many useful features, including support for SSL, TLS, and SMTP-AUTH. The fact that these additional features are bundled together adds a level of convenience to this option, if the other features of `mailfront` are used. Because `mailfront`, Vermeulen's patch, and the `stunnel` program all operate within the same security region as `qmail-smtpd`—i.e. as a user with restricted permissions—they are subject to essentially the same caveats: a security breach in one has the same impact as a breach within `qmail-smtpd`. But by operating with the same security restrictions as `qmail-smtpd`, they all benefit from qmail's privilege-separation architecture in the same way that `qmail-smtpd` does: if exploited, they run as a user with insufficient permissions to do very much. Capitalizing on such an exploit is much more difficult. This is not to say that any of them has a history of security flaws, but merely that their history of security is not as long (Vermeulen's patch and `mailfront` both have flawless security track records).

Using a patch to add SSL support to *tcpserver* is an interesting idea because it has the potential to undermine the security design of the qmail architecture on most UNIX systems. Since listening to the network requires *root* permissions, *tcpserver* normally runs briefly as the *root* user, and thus has sufficient permissions to do virtually anything. (Some UNIX variants, such as SELinux, allow permissions to be highly customized, and so *tcpserver* can technically be run as a user with permission to listen to the network but without sufficient permissions to do anything else.) This is usually acceptable for two reasons: *tcpserver* drops the *root* power quickly, and its task is extremely simple. Because *tcpserver* does not attempt to understand or interpret any of the network traffic, it is virtually impossible to exploit.

However, implementing SSL within `tcpserver` means that `tcpserver` performs a more complex job and interprets untrusted user (or attacker) input. This is risky, which is precisely why `qmail-smtpd` runs with restricted permissions. Oppermann's patch is very careful to only use OpenSSL after `tcpserver` has dropped its *root* privileges. If Oppermann was not as careful, the patch could have become a severe liability. Other patches that perform a similar task may not be as careful.

When Sending Email

It is important to note that `mailfront`, Oppermann's patch to `tcpserver`, and `stunnel` enable qmail to receive encrypted connections but not to make encrypted connections to other SMTP servers. These options only enable clients to send mail to the qmail server in an encrypted form. If the goal, however, is to make qmail use encryption for its outbound connections, then none of these three solutions is up to the task. Frederick Vermeulen's patch, on the other hand, is the only mainstream addition to qmail that provides this ability. With Vermeulen's patch, `qmail-remote` uses and understands the extended SMTP EHLO semantics: it tests recipient servers to determine whether they support TLS and uses TLS encryption if they do. With this patch, `qmail-remote` also automatically uses encryption when connecting to port 465 (the SMTPS port) on any server; this behavior is specified by the `smtproutes` file.

The primary drawback to Frederick Vermeulen's patch is its size—it patches both `qmail-smtpd` and `qmail-remote` and alters and adds a significant amount of code to both. Although it has been tested in many places for a long time, it might still contain bugs. In addition, these extensive code additions have more potential to conflict with other qmail patches. For example, one of the most common situations for encryption is when using SMTP-AUTH, to protect the passwords transmitted during authentication. Most of the SMTP-AUTH patches, however, conflict with Vermeulen's patch. Because this is so common, a small segment at the beginning of the patch can be removed to allow it to cooperate with the popular SMTP-AUTH patches. Despite this concession to compatibility, the patch still conflicts with, or confuses, many other unrelated patches to `qmail-smtpd`, and these conflicts usually require manual resolution.

Mailing Lists

One of the most important and most common tasks that mail servers do is the distribution of email via mailing lists. Many organizations rely on mailing lists not only to reach their customers or constituents, but also to provide a means of communication within the organization or a group within that organization. The complexity and difficulty of this task varies depending on the number of recipients on a given list, and the level of automatic maintenance required. Choosing a mailing list management strategy or software package requires careful consideration of the needs and goals of the mailing list or lists.

Lightweight vs. Heavyweight

The most basic form of sending an email to a mailing list is simply sending an email with multiple addresses in the To header. This technique is easy, simple, and for a small number of recipients, it makes perfect sense. The intermediate level is the alias-based mailing list. This is akin to having a group in an address book that the email server accesses. With this, one sends an email to all of the addresses listed in the alias by simply sending an email to a special email address representing that group. For example, in qmail, creating the file ~alias/.qmail-mylist creates the address mylist@yourdomain.com (assuming the qmail server's name is yourdomain.com). This file is filled with addresses (one per line), each of which receives a copy of every message sent to mylist@yourdomain.com. This is a lightweight mailing list, because it is so simple: it is defined in a single file and maintained by manually editing that file.

The problem with such a list is someone (who has permissions to edit ~alias/.qmail files) must maintain the list's membership. For small mailing lists or lists whose membership does not change often, this is not usually a problem. However, once the membership of a list gets large (over a hundred people, for example), maintenance of this file becomes a significant chore. It is often desirable to establish a mailing list where people can join or leave without involving the mailing-list administrator. This self-serve option requires software and that capability distinguishes a heavyweight list from a lightweight list.

Heavyweight list management software, of course, frequently includes other convenient features, including the abilities to easily archive all list messages, to prevent non-subscribers from posting, to allow message moderation, to provide some users with daily digests of all list messages, and many others. Examples of popular heavyweight list management software packages that work with qmail include ezmlm (http://cr.yp.to/ezmlm.html) by qmail's author, Dr. Bernstein; ezmlm-idx (http://www.ezmlm.org/) by Bruce Guenter (based on ezmlm); and GNU Mailman (http://www.gnu.org/software/mailman/).

Speed vs. Size

When comparing mailing-list manager software, important details to evaluate include:

- How many messages can the mailing-list manager handle per day or at a time?
- How does the mailing-list manager perform under load?
- How does the manager store its recipient list, and how quickly can it find a particular recipient?

The most fundamental question regarding mailing lists is: what are the speed limitations of posting to the list? In many cases, the real limitation is the outbound network bandwidth from the mail server: only a limited number of messages can be transmitted over the same wires at one time. This is not always the case. Poor software design can cause mismanagement or inefficient use of bandwidth. For example, the email server may use too much bandwidth retrying undeliverable messages or the mailing list management software may spend too much time managing itself and not spend enough time queuing messages for delivery.

Member Management

One of the tasks mailing list management software often performs is automatic handling of email bounces to detect and remove undeliverable email addresses from its membership list. In a list with tens of thousands of members, the likelihood of some being undeliverable is rather high. When a bounce message comes back informing the list of a delivery failure, it must locate that recipient in its internal records and record the bounce. In a list of tens of thousands of names, simply searching through the list linearly takes too much time. And, of course, every undeliverable message causes a recipient lookup. If the mailing list is restricted such that only subscribers can post, every single message sent also requires a search of the membership rolls to verify that the sender of the message is indeed subscribed. At the same time, every posting requires that all of the addresses be collected and fed to the email server. For very large, very busy mailing lists or mailing-list servers, allowing a subscription request, a bounce, or a membership check to take more than a second of CPU time is too much.

The most popular list management software packages used with qmail store their subscriber lists differently. `ezmlm` and `ezmlm-idx` store user lists in hashed directories of files, while GNU Mailman stores its user lists in binary database files. The database files are faster than hashed files if they're kept in memory, while the hashed files are often (but not always) faster than database files if the database files cannot be kept in memory. Hashed files, however, are editable by hand if necessary, while GNU Mailman's binary database format cannot be reconstructed or hand-edited easily.

Efficiency under Load

The number of processes that handle each posting to each list is a common way of comparing mailing-list efficiency. The idea is the more processes required, the greater the load placed on the server for each message. For email servers with minimal amounts of mailing-list traffic, this is essentially irrelevant, but in high-load situations, this is much more important. `ezmlm` and `ezmlm-idx` invoke multiple programs (typically, three or four) every time a message is sent to the list. Different numbers of programs are used depending on the enabled options for that particular list. Handing the posted messages to the email server for delivery requires another two processes (`qmail-inject` and `qmail-queue`). GNU Mailman, on the other hand, invokes only two programs (`preline` and `mailman`) to receive every message, and another three (`sendmail`, `qmail-inject`, and `qmail-queue`) to queue messages for delivery. Thus, if large volumes of email are sent, `ezmlm` and `ezmlm-idx` spawn more programs than GNU Mailman and impose more program-loading overhead on the server. On the other hand, the programs spawned by `ezmlm` and `ezmlm-idx` are all small and simple. GNU Mailman's `mailman` program is a wrapper around a Python program. Because Python is an interpreted language and its interpreter is large and must parse the entire input program before doing any useful work, starting up a Python program takes longer than a simpler, compiled program. To mitigate the overhead of starting multiple large Python programs, GNU Mailman has a daemon (`qrunner`) to handle most of the operations of the mailing lists, allowing the `mailman` program to be simpler and merely submit job requests to `qrunner`. In any case, the efficiency differences between the `ezmlm`/`ezmlm-idx` and GNU Mailman cannot be treated as simply a case of one starting more programs than the other. Not only is the overhead per process different depending on the process, but on many servers, the cost of invoking processes is greatly overshadowed by other costs, such as the cost of bounce message handling.

Variable Envelope Return Path

Not all recipients can be contacted every time mailing list messages are distributed. It is ordinarily desirable to track which members of a list have not received messages, and for what reason. For example, if a given address no longer exists, the mailing-list manager could warn the list administrator and temporarily remove that address from the distribution list. This procedure is complicated by the fact that mailing-list software cannot know whether mail was delivered immediately. If the software is to automatically monitor delivery success, it must receive and interpret bounce messages.

While receiving bounce messages is relatively easy by simply setting the envelope sender address of each outbound list message to a special list-specific email address, reliably interpreting those bounce messages is difficult. Because the format and language of bounce messages varies, reliably extracting the reason for the bounce and even the recipient responsible is challenging.

To address this problem, a technique exists to encode the recipient of a list message in the return address. There are many ways of doing it, but the formalized technique is known as **Variable Envelope Return Path** (VERP). Messages are normally fed to a mail server (such as qmail) with a single sender and one or more recipients. In order to give every recipient a unique sender, a new copy of the message body normally must be given to the mail server for each recipient. For small lists this is not a problem, but for large lists, this presents a storage and efficiency dilemma, as the queue must track and store each message separately.

The solution, in this case, is VERP and transferring the responsibility of changing the sender of each message from the mailing-list software to the email-server software. By standardizing the method of encoding a recipient into the sending address, the encoding can occur at any location, including within the email server. In this case, `qmail-remote` is either patched or wrapped so messages from mailing lists (with a special return address to indicate that VERP encoding should be employed) are rewritten as they exit the queue, rather than as they enter the queue. This drastically reduces the overhead of VERP while maintaining its functionality. Both `ezmlm` and GNU Mailman support VERP. `ezmlm` uses it by default; and GNU Mailman can be configured to do so. Neither one relies on an implementation in the email server (qmail), though Frederik Lindberg has written a patch (`http://www.ezmlm.org/archive/patches/qmail-verh-0.06.tar.gz`) to both qmail and `ezmlm` that allows them to cooperate this way. GNU Mailman usually restricts its use of VERP to probe messages. This avoids using extra resources for each normal mailing list message without relying on the email server to implement particular support for VERP. However, this can lead to a failure to detect some failed deliveries.

Integration with Qmail

Not all mailing-list software works optimally with the qmail architecture because mailing-list software frequently is tightly bound to specific email-server software to take best advantage of its features. For example, the popular mailing list management software Majordomo was originally designed specifically for the Sendmail email server, and relies on the details of the Sendmail aliasing system. Since qmail can be made to interpret Sendmail alias files, and since Majordomo can be altered to create qmail aliases, they can be made to work together, though not generally as efficiently and/or conveniently as software designed for use with qmail. (It is expected that Majordomo 2.0 will support qmail directly, but work on Majordomo 2.0 has been in progress since even before qmail was written and as of this writing does not have a set release date.) Of the three software packages recommended here—`ezmlm`, `ezmlm-idx`, and GNU Mailman—the first two are designed explicitly for qmail (though they can work with servers like Postfix). Because of this, `ezmlm` and `ezmlm-idx` are easy to install and get running with qmail. GNU Mailman, on the other hand, is designed to work with a broad range of email servers and therefore requires *glue* between itself and the email server.

For example, GNU Mailman establishes several standard email addresses for each of its mailing lists (similar to `ezmlm` and `ezmlm-idx`) to handle administrative requests, bounces, and other specific tasks. Enabling delivery of mailing-list addresses with these software packages requires either several `.qmail` files (one per address) or a way to deliver all of the mailing list messages to a single address prefix and a script that delivers messages to their intended destinations. `ezmlm` and `ezmlm-idx` handle `.qmail` file creation themselves. A common approach with GNU Mailman is to create a virtual domain for all GNU Mailman mailing lists (e.g. `lists.example.com`) and put a `.qmail-default` file in that domain's home directory that directs `qmail-local` to feed messages to a script (a Python version is provided with GNU Mailman). This script determines the original destination address and then calls `mailman` with the correct arguments. While this script (glue) makes management of GNU Mailman mailing lists less involved, it also increases the overhead required to process every message posted to GNU Mailman lists.

Web Interface

One of the most popular and visible features of mailing lists is their ability to keep an archive of messages distributed on the list, and make this archive available from a web browser. GNU Mailman makes this relatively easy because its entire management system is based around a web-browser interface. Making list archives available via the Web requires only enabling the archives and properly configuring the web server. Providing a web interface for `ezmlm` archives requires more work because it does not come with such an interface. The easiest option is the ezmlm-www software (`http://ezmlm-www.sourceforge.net/`), a Perl-based CGI script. `ezmlm-idx` adds more extensive web support to `ezmlm`. `ezmlm-idx` comes with a program called `ezmlm-cgi` that—when properly configured—allows web-based browsing of list archives. However, its interface is not particularly user friendly. A more attractive alternative is ezmlm-browse (`http://untroubled.org/ezmlm-browse/`) written by Bruce Guenter. Because Guenter wrote both `ezmlm-browse` and `ezmlm-idx`, they work well together.

It is often convenient to administer, not just browse, mailing lists from a web browser, executing administrative tasks such as moderation and changing settings. `ezmlm` and `ezmlm-idx` make it possible to do advanced administrative tasks entirely via email, but a web browser is typically more convenient. The GNU Mailman software is controlled entirely from its built-in web interface—many configuration details can be set only from its web interface. `ezmlm` and `ezmlm-idx`, however, are both oriented primarily towards command-line-based configuration, though they can be configured via email. The ezmlm-web software package (`https://systemausfall.org/toolforge/ezmlm-web/`), however, provides a web-based interface for configuring both `ezmlm` and `ezmlm-idx`.

Summary

This chapter has covered two common needs of qmail administrators: encryption and mailing-list management. This discussion has built upon the knowledge of qmail architecture presented in the preceding chapters, as examples of how to approach important features with qmail's architecture in mind. The next chapter will cover how to optimize a qmail server for particular environments, and how to maintain a qmail server over time.

8
Administration, Optimization, and Monitoring

This chapter covers the two most important tools an administrator needs when maintaining a qmail server over the long term: analyzing the log files to locate problems, and on that basis finding ways to improve qmail's performance.

The Log Files

When analyzing qmail's operation for almost any purpose, the first place to begin looking is in qmail's log files. In a standard qmail setup, there are two sources of log files: one for *qmail-send* and one for *qmail-smtpd*. By default, these contain both useful information for tracking down individual messages and useful information for analyzing qmail's performance.

The log output of both *qmail-send* and *qmail-smtpd* is organized in a simple way, though it can easily become confusing.

The Basic qmail-smtpd Log

The *qmail-smtpd* log file is the simpler of the two because *qmail-smtpd* does not generate log output. The *qmail-smtpd* log records the output of *tcpserver*. *tcpserver* generates five log entries for every connection:

1. When the connection opens, it logs the current number of connections and the maximum number of connections.
2. When the connection opens, it logs the client and the **process-identifier (PID)** of the child process handling that connection.
3. After all the necessary client information is collected, it logs the information and the decision whether to allow the connection.

4. After the child process (e.g. `qmail-smtpd`) exits, it records the child process's return value.

5. When the connection closes, it records the current and the maximum number of connections.

The following is an example of the five log entries:

```
tcpserver: status: 1/20
tcpserver: pid 13609 from 1.2.3.4
tcpserver: ok 13609 example.com:1.2.3.5:25 example2.net:1.2.3.4:joe:2985
tcpserver: end 13609 status 0
tcpserver: status: 0/20
```

The first and last entries indicate that a maximum of twenty connections are available at one time. In the first entry `tcpserver` reports that one of these twenty is in use, and in the last entry `tcpserver` reports no active connections.

The second log entry reports that the PID of the child process handling the new connection is `13609` and the IP address of the connected client is `1.2.3.4`.

The third log entry is of the form:

decision pid localname:localIP:localport remotename:remoteIP:remoteuser:remoteport

The "decision" string indicates whether the connection attempt will be allowed to continue (`ok`) or will be closed immediately (`deny`). Much of the remaining information is stored in environment variables accessible by the child process. In terms of these environment variables, this log entry is in the form:

decision pid $TCPLOCALHOST:$TCPLOCALIP:$TCPLOCALPORT $TCPREMOTEHOST: $TCPREMOTEIP:$TCPREMOTEINFO:$TCPREMOTEPORT

Thus, the decision by the child process `13609` is to allow (`ok`) the connection from the user *joe* on the computer `example2.net` with IP address `1.2.3.4` connecting from port `2985` to the local machine `example.com` listening on IP address `1.2.3.5` on port `25` (the standard SMTP port). Not all of this information about the remote host is necessarily available. For example, if `tcpserver` was told not to look up the remote host's DNS name (with the `-H` flag) or could not find that information, the TCPREMOTEHOST will be missing. And if `tcpserver` was told not to use the ident protocol to ask the remote host for the username responsible for the connection (with the `-R` flag, which is currently the standard practice since many servers drop ident connections, which slows down connection attempts) or could not retrieve that information, the TCPREMOTEINFO will be missing.

Without that information, the above example would look like:

```
tcpserver: ok 13609 example.com:1.2.3.5:25 :1.2.3.4::2985
```

The fourth log entry is deceptively simple. The *end* tag signifies it is reporting the return value of the child, but the status it reports is the result of the `waitpid()` (or `wait3()`) system call, not the literal return value of the application. To extract useful information from this value, if it is non-zero, the system administrator must process it according to the particulars of the operating system in use. The man page(s) for the `waitpid()` and `wait3()` system calls contain information about how to do this. In any case, a status of `0` means the child exited successfully and did not report an error.

Expanding the qmail-smtpd Log

While the *tcpserver* log messages are sufficient for most purposes, it can be useful to record more information about each connection. As is usually the case with qmail, there are two ways of doing this: patching *qmail-smtpd*, and wrapping *qmail-smtpd*. The choice depends on the user's needs.

The typical wrapper around *qmail-smtpd* for logging purposes is the `recordio` program, part of the ucspi-tcp package. This program serves as a tap: it pipes information between the client and *qmail-smtpd*, and writes a copy of the communication back and forth to standard error (file descriptor 2). In most *tcpserver* scripts, this is then re-directed to standard output (file descriptor 1) so it ends up in the log files. `recordio` records everything and is useful for advanced debugging of network connections. When combined with *multilog*'s ability to filter log messages, `recordio` is a convenient way of logging SMTP errors. For example, a technique to invoke *multilog* (such as in the /service/qmail-smtpd/log/run file) to filter out most of `recordio`'s output but still log any error messages that *qmail-smtpd* generates is:

```
#!/bin/sh
exec setuidgid qmaill multilog \
    '-* * > *' \
    '-* * < *' \
    '+* * > 5*' \
    '+* * > 4*' \
    t /var/log/qmail/smtpd
```

The extra lines in this example are *multilog* filter commands. The first two instruct *multilog* not to log any `recordio` output lines. The third directs *multilog* to log the `recordio` output lines involving permanent SMTP errors (all beginning with an error code 5xx), and the fourth directs *multilog* to log the `recordio` output lines involving temporary SMTP errors (all beginning with an error code 4xx).

While `recordio` or similar software is very useful, it is not always succinct or particularly efficient. Another common method of expanding the `qmail-smtpd` log files is patching `qmail-smtpd`. There are several patches available for that. One of the simplest, written by Kyle Wheeler (http://www.memoryhole.net/qmail/logging.patch), reports every decision `qmail-smtpd` makes as well as some of the information about the incoming email and the client. Log entries generated by this patch are in the following form:

`qmail-smtpd`: decision (reason): mailfrom from remoteIP to firstrecipient helo helostring

If there is no relevant reason, the "(*reason*):" is left out of the log entry. The following log entries are two examples generated by this patch:

```
qmail-smtpd: message rejected (mail server permanently
rejected message (#5.3.0)): spammer@somewhere.com from 1.2.3.4 to
me@mydomain.com helo spammersayshi

qmail-smtpd: message accepted: friend@example.com from 1.2.3.9 to
me@mydomain.com helo example.com
```

Dr. Erwin Hoffman's SPAMCONTROL patch (http://www.fehcom.de/qmail/spamcontrol.html) provides more flexible, extensible logging from `qmail-smtpd`. The format of log messages from this patch is:

action::type::condition: information

It is extensible in that future changes to `qmail-smtpd`'s behavior are all categorized and succinctly summarized by this format.

The Basic qmail-send Log

The log output generated by `qmail-send` is complicated because each message generates a different number of log entries and tracking a single message through a busy server's log easily becomes confusing. Each log entry, by itself, is simple and straightforward. A full description of every possible `qmail-send` log message is available in the qmail-log man page, but it is generally simpler than as described. Every message generates a minimum of seven log entries:

1. When a new message is injected into the queue for delivery, it logs the discovery of the message and the inode number of the message body in the queue. Every file in a UNIX system has a unique number, called the **inode number**. `qmail-send` renames messages to have the same name as the message's inode number.

2. When a new message is injected into the queue for delivery, it logs the size, sender, long-term message identifier (aka "qp"), and the UID of the process that called `qmail-queue` to enqueue the message.

3. When a delivery attempt begins, it logs the delivery attempt number, the message inode number, whether the attempt is local or remote, and the email address of the recipient.

4. When a delivery attempt begins, it logs the number of ongoing local delivery attempts, the maximum number of concurrent local delivery attempts allowed, the number of ongoing remote delivery attempts, and the maximum number of concurrent remote delivery attempts allowed.

5. When a delivery attempt finishes, it logs whether the delivery was successful, and any status messages generated by the attempt. If the messages have multiple lines, the lines are concatenated and separated by a slash (/). Any whitespace in the messages is replaced with an underscore (_).

6. When a delivery attempt finishes, it logs the number of ongoing local delivery attempts, the maximum number of concurrent local delivery attempts allowed, the number of ongoing remote delivery attempts, and the maximum number of concurrent remote delivery attempts allowed.

7. When all delivery attempts for a message are completed successfully (or the message has been in the queue too long), it logs the message's inode number.

Here is an example of these seven log entries:

```
new msg 96025
info msg 96025: bytes 9956 from <user@example.com> qp 16296 uid 101
starting delivery 1461: msg 96025 to local me@mydomain.com
status: local 1/10 remote 0/20
delivery 1461: success: did_1+0+2
status: local 0/10 remote 0/20
end msg 96025
```

The first entry records that a new message, stored in a file with the inode number 96025, was discovered in the queue. The second entry records that the message using inode 96025 is 9956 bytes long, has a return address of user@example.com, has a long-term queue identifier of 16296, and was queued by a process with the UID of 101 (probably the UID used by *qmail-smtpd*, *qmaild*). The third entry declares delivery attempt 1461 has begun, qmail will attempt to deliver the message stored in the file whose inode number is 96025, and the delivery attempt is to the local address me@mydomain.com. The fourth entry reports one local attempt is currently happening and a maximum of ten local attempts and twenty remote attempts are permissible.

The fifth entry reports the delivery succeeded, and the delivery agent (`qmail-local`) printed out information indicating it delivered the message to one local mailbox, requeued the message for zero other addresses, and piped the message to two programs. The sixth entry reports there are no ongoing delivery attempts. Finally, the seventh entry reports `qmail-send` is done with that message and the message has been removed from the queue.

Many things can complicate these logs. Obviously when there are multiple deliveries occurring simultaneously and new messages are injected frequently, these log entries are interleaved. Emails with multiple recipients have their recipients listed with each delivery attempt, rather than as a collection together. Failed delivery attempts leave the message in the queue so qmail will attempt additional deliveries later. Connecting delivery attempts to their related message initially is a confusing task.

The three key pieces of information connecting these log entries together are the message inode number, the delivery attempt number, and the long-lived message identifier (qp). In the previous example these are, respectively, 96025, 1461, and 16296. The inode number (96025) is determined by the filesystem on which qmail's queue is stored. It is important to recognize that while only one message has a given inode number at one time these numbers are reused very quickly on most UNIX filesystems. It is not unusual to see sequential messages using the same inode number. Because of inode reuse, searching for a specific message with just that is difficult. To assist with this, qmail also has a "long-lived" message identifier: the process identifier (PID) of the `qmail-queue` instance that enqueued the message. Note that PIDs are also reused periodically, and the reuse rate depends both on the operating system and how busy it is. Most UNIX operating systems assign PIDs in a cycle of approximately 65,536 processes. Thus, the "long-lived" identifier theoretically *can* be reused immediately, just as the inode number can be, but it is just less likely. More to the point, it is also possible for two messages in the queue to share a "long-lived" identifier, though that is also unlikely. Finally, a sequential counter in `qmail-send` determines the delivery number. This counter is initialized to zero whenever `qmail-send` starts and can count as high as 4,294,967,296 on most 32-bit systems or 18,446,744,073,709,551,616 on most 64-bit systems before resetting back to zero. Although this counter can and will reset if qmail processes enough mail, the most common reason for duplicate delivery numbers is `qmail-send` being restarted. (On a 32-bit system, even if qmail attempted 100 deliveries every second, it would take more than a year for a delivery number to be reused. On a 64-bit system, it would take more than five billion years to reuse the same delivery number.)

Basic Analysis

The `qmail-send` and `qmail-smtpd` logs easily demonstrate how busy the system is. Both logs provide a status indication of how many messages are handled concurrently at any given time and the limit on this concurrency. These status log entries combined with their timestamp give a picture of the load over time. Tracing a message through the system is relatively easy to do by hand: first, find the point where the message is injected into the queue, use its inode number to find the message's delivery attempts then use the delivery numbers of these attempts to locate the results of these attempts. When using a script to determine the same information, the potential reuse of the various identification numbers makes correct analysis rather tricky.

qmailanalog

To assist with analyzing the `qmail-send` logs, Dr. Bernstein wrote the qmailanalog software package (http://cr.yp.to/qmailanalog.html). This package excels in generating summaries of the `qmail-send` logs and has some limited ability to locate specific messages in the logs. Unfortunately, qmailanalog relies on having the timestamps in `qmail-send`'s logs encoded in a rarely-used format known as **Temps Atomique International**, or **International Atomic Time (TAI)**. Syslog uses a human-readable format, and `multilog` generates timestamps in tai64n format — a more recent variation of the TAI format. There are two ways to address the problem: either patch qmailanalog to understand `multilog`'s tai64n timestamps — such as with the patch written by Charles Cazabon (http://pyropus.ca/software/misc/qmailanalog-date-patch) — or feed the log files through a program that converts tai64n timestamps into TAI timestamps. One such conversion program is the `tai64n2tai` program in the qlogtools package written by Bruce Guenter (http://untroubled.org/qlogtools/).

qmailanalog first transforms the `qmail-send` logs into a succinct format with the `matchup` program from the package. This more compact, machine-readable format is input to the rest of the qmailanalog programs to generate human-readable summaries of that data.

The `matchup` program was designed to be particularly useful when used periodically to process logs and has a feature to track messages whose log entries are split between log files. Specifically, it prints partial delivery data to file descriptor 5. This can be somewhat annoying when the program is used alone, as it complains and refuses to run if that file descriptor is not already open. It is important to be aware, however, that when used alone, `matchup` will ignore deliveries starting before the analyzed log file begins and that have not finished before the log file ends.

A common way to use *matchup* to process all the current logs is:

```
cat /var/log/qmail/send/@* /var/log/qmail/send/current | \
    tai64n2tai | \
    matchup 5>/dev/null >matchup_output
```

In this example, the file matchup_output can subsequently be used as input to the other programs in the qmailanalog package. qmailanalog and *matchup* may also be used periodically to process newly rotated log files. For example:

```
touch /tmp/matchup-prev
cat /tmp/matchup-prev /var/log/qmail/send/@*   | \
    tai64n2tai | \
    matchup 5>/tmp/matchup-next >matchup_output
mv /tmp/matchup-next /tmp/matchup-prev
```

This shell script isn't completely sufficient because it doesn't keep track of which rotated logs have been processed and which have not. *multilog* has the ability to process logs through an external program as they are rotated, which is ideal for qmailanalog's design. An example script to use is:

```
#!/bin/sh
touch /tmp/matchup-prev
cat /tmp/matchup-prev - | tai64n2tai | \
    matchup 5>/tmp/matchup-next >matchup_output
mv /tmp/matchup-next /tmp/matchup-prev
```

An example *multilog* run file, based on *qmail-send*'s logging run file, that uses such a script (assuming that script is saved in /usr/bin/matchup.sh) is:

```
#!/bin/sh
exec /usr/bin/setuidgid qmaill /usr/bin/multilog t \
    '!/usr/bin/matchup.sh' /var/log/qmail/send
```

In the previous examples, the file matchup_output can subsequently be used as input to the other programs in the qmailanalog package. The summary programs have names beginning with the letter z, and they behave as follows:

- *zddist* prints a histogram of delivery delay time by percentage of messages. This demonstrates, for example, what percentage of messages were delivered in less than a second, what percentage were delivered in less than a minute, and so forth.

- *zdeferrals* prints a list of the reasons for which messages were deferred, how many were deferred for that reason, and how long those messages took to be deferred.

- *zfailures* prints a list of all the reasons due to which message delivery failed, how many failed for that reason, and how long those messages took to fail.

- *zoverall* prints a summary of the logs, including how many messages were delivered, how many attempts failed, how many attempts were deferred, average time messages spent in the queue, how many bytes were processed, and several other statistics.

- *zrecipients* prints a list of all the recipients of qmail's delivery attempts, how many messages were addressed to each, how many tries it took to deliver those messages, how long those attempts took, and how many bytes were delivered successfully to each recipient.

- *zrhosts* prints a list of all the hosts receiving qmail's delivery attempts, how many messages were attempted, how many attempts it took to deliver those messages, and how many bytes were delivered to each host.

- *zrxdelay* prints a list of all the recipients of qmail's delivery attempts, sorted by how long on an average it took to deliver to that recipient (successfully or not).

- *zsenders* prints a list of the sender addresses for the email qmail attempted to deliver along with the number of messages, bytes sent, bytes successfully received, number of recipients, number of delivery attempts, and amount of time each sender's mail took to deliver.

- *zsendmail* prints a version of the log in a format very similar to that used by *sendmail*.

- *zsuccesses* prints a list of all messages given by successful delivery attempts (note that many successful deliveries either have no message or have a unique message).

- *zsuids* prints a list of UIDs that sent messages along with the number of messages, bytes, successfully-delivered bytes, number of recipients, number of delivery attempts, and amount of time used for those delivery attempts for each UID.

The qmailanalog package also provides some programs for selecting only certain messages. The output of these selection programs uses the same format as the output of the *matchup* program, and is fed to one of the summary programs listed above. The selection programs have names beginning with the letter x, and function as follows:

- *xsender* selects all messages sent by the address given on the command line. For example, this program could be used like this:

```
cat matchup_output | xsender user@domain.com | zoverall
```

- *xrecipient* selects all messages delivered to the address given on the command line. This recipient must be both the final address (i.e. after any transformations specified by the control/virtualdomains file), and prepended by the type of delivery that would be made to it (either remote or local). For example, this program would be used like this:

```
cat matchup_output | xrecipient local.user@domain.com | zoverall
```

If domain.com is a virtual domain, then it would be used like this:

```
cat matchup_output |\
    xrecipient local.domainvirtualuser-user@domain.com | zoverall
```

- *xqp* selects messages with the long-lived identifier given on the command line. Remember, this identifier is reused and so is a convenience, not a guarantee of selecting only a single message. This program would be used like this:

```
cat matchup_output | xqp 16296 | zoverall
```

The other programs in the qmailanalog package are used by the summary programs to generate their output and can be safely ignored.

Identifying Problems

There are two cases where the qmail administrator uses the logs to look for problems: to search for the cause of a specific manifested problem or to monitor the logs for potential problems.

Finding the cause of a problem generally depends on the problem's specifics. For example, "mail is slow" can be caused by many things—an overloaded server, a full filesystem, unnecessary DNS or ident lookups by *tcpserver*, a corrupted queue trigger file, and so forth. The cause of the problem may not be listed in the logs, but reviewing the logs for anything out of the ordinary is advised.

However, the logs are the best place to start looking when a message was not delivered or was delivered multiple times, or something similar. From the date the message was queued, the sender, and the recipients, one can accurately isolate the relevant *qmail-send* log messages and determine what happened to that message.

Monitoring the logs to automatically detect problems is a more complex task, and there are many approaches. Looking through the logs for anything that starts with the strings "alert:", "internal error:", "qmail-clean", "trouble", "unable", or "unknown" is a good start. Unless something is seriously wrong with the system, these error messages should never occur. Delivery errors of some kind are a more common problem. Periodically checking the most common causes of error—such as with the qmailanalog package—is a good preventative measure. Most of the time, the failures are innocuous, such as non-existent recipients and poorly configured destination hosts, but if messages begin failing with unusually high frequency, they deserve a closer examination. The following is an example script that emails the top ten most common recent (recent enough to still be in /var/log/qmail/send/current) causes of delivery failure to the address me@mydomain.com:

```
#!/bin/sh
cat /var/log/qmail/send/current | \
    tai64n2tai | \
    matchup 5>/dev/null | \
    zfailures | \
    awk 'NR>8' | sort -n -r | awk 'NR<11' | \
    mail -s 'Mail Failures' me@mydomain.com
```

It seems odd to monitor an email system with email, but if the system administrator cannot receive email, notification that something is wrong is probably redundant.

Making It Faster

While qmail is generally fast at processing, routing, and delivering email, in some circumstances its speed can be improved. This involves either tailoring qmail to take full advantage of the available hardware or improving the hardware. The best strategy depends on the situation.

Calculating Your Limits

It is important to first determine what speed is theoretically possible before analyzing qmail to find problems and improve speed. Qmail's ability to deliver email quickly is limited by several physical realities, including:

- Network bandwidth
- Disk-drive bandwidth
- Server memory

For example, if an email server is connected to the Internet by a 320kbps link (or 40 kilobytes per second) and if the average email is ten kilobytes, then only 4 emails can be transmitted per second. That means 240 messages per minute, and 14,400 messages per hour, as long as there are no other forms of traffic on the network and (inaccurately) assuming there is no SMTP-protocol overhead. Thus, delivering a mailing-list post to 100,000 recipients takes approximately seven hours, and delivering a mailing-list post to 2,400 recipients takes nothing less than ten minutes, no matter how efficient qmail is.

Accounting for disk-drive bandwidth is harder because a lot of it depends on the filesystem in use and the queue split factor. However, in order to be robust, qmail tries to ensure that files in the queue are written to disk (and not simply cached), circumventing many of the shortcuts that disk drives take to appear fast.

Server memory is an important factor because it influences the configuration of qmail. For example, when receiving email from the network, there is an instance of `qmail-smtpd` for each connection. When `qmail-smtpd` queues a message, it runs `qmail-queue` (or `qmail-queue`'s wrapper) and waits for them to finish. Thus, the amount of memory each instance of `qmail-smtpd` consumes plus the amount of memory each instance of `qmail-queue` (or its wrappers) consumes constitutes a natural limit on the number of instances that can run concurrently. This is particularly important when adding features to `qmail-smtpd` (i.e. with a patch) and wrapping `qmail-queue`. While `qmail-smtpd` and `qmail-queue` are normally very lightweight, many of their wrappers or patches increase their memory footprint significantly. For example, Perl is often used by `qmail-queue` wrappers, and can use around 20MB of memory per instance. On a server with a gigabyte of RAM, this places a natural limit of approximately 50 concurrent instances of a Perl-based wrapper, leaving little memory for `qmail-smtpd`, `qmail-queue`, and any other processes on the server (such as `qmail-send` or the operating system). Of course, swap space increases the available memory and allows more processes to run concurrently, but severely degrades the performance of the system.

In addition to the physical limits, qmail's configuration imposes limits on performance as well. The most important of these are:

- The queue "split" factor
- Remote and local delivery parallelism
- `qmail-smtpd` parallelism
- The use of an external `qmail-todo` program

These limits are useful, but can be too limiting in some circumstances. For example, limiting the number of concurrent `qmail-smtpd` instances allows an administrator to prevent the system from using swap space and limits the potential impact of a denial-of-service attack on the system. Limitations, obviously, prevent qmail from overusing (or abusing) the system's resources, but can also prevent it from benefiting from all the available resources.

Finding Bottlenecks

When attempting to speed up a system as complex as qmail, the basic task is to first locate the part of the system responsible for limiting the speed. This bottleneck can be any of the limits mentioned previously, but identifying which one can require serious investigating skills.

Beyond qmail's configuration and the natural limitations of the system itself, qmail is limited also by the other systems it uses. The most common example of this is the DNS system. Qmail, like all email servers, relies heavily on DNS for routing email. Without a local DNS cache, or with an overloaded or poorly performing local DNS cache, qmail's speed of routing email is drastically reduced.

Concurrency

The first thing to examine if qmail is behaving unacceptably is the log files. Both *qmail-smtpd*'s and *qmail-send*'s log output include indications of the system's concurrency along with the currently configured limitation on that concurrency. The relevant *qmail-smtpd* log entries look like this:

```
tcpserver: status: 0/20
```

The status number's format is "number currently running"/"number allowed to run"; in this case 20 instances are allowed, and 0 are currently running. If the log had many entries as shown below, *tcpserver* is consequently running up against its current limits, resulting in a performance bottleneck:

```
tcpserver: status: 20/20
```

It also means that many people are unable to contact the server when they desire, meaning mail is being delayed. To fix this, increase the limit on the number of *qmail-smtpd* instances (with the *-c* flag) within *tcpserver*. In addition, make sure the machine has enough RAM to support a larger number of concurrent connections.

The *qmail-send* logs reporting a similar limitation appear as follows. A server that is not busy has many log entries such as:

```
status: local 0/10 remote 0/20
```

On the other hand, a busier server will report higher concurrency levels. These log entries mean the same as the status entries in the *qmail-smtpd* logs, though they record two different limits. The first number pair refers to limits on the number of concurrent instances of *qmail-local*, and the second refers to limits on concurrent instances of *qmail-remote*. As explained while examining the *qmail-smtpd* logs, if the numbers on either side of the slash are frequently the same, then either local deliveries or remote deliveries are restricted, and increasing the corresponding limit would positively impact performance. Also, as with *qmail-smtpd*, before increasing the limits (via control/concurrencylocal for local deliveries and control/concurrencyremote for remote deliveries) make certain that the system has enough memory for the increased concurrency. The worst case peak-use scenario is for all programs to run with their maximum allowed concurrency.

Resource Starvation

Beyond the logs, potential bottlenecks are found using other tools. For example, if the system's load average is high (i.e. greater than 2.0), qmail is spending a long time waiting for the disk, and either a faster disk or a better queue layout (or both) will improve qmail's performance. The `top` utility can determine the load. If the system uses a lot of memory, especially if it is using swap space, the high load may be a result of insufficient RAM, and this can be determined using `top`. To alleviate insufficient RAM problems, either add more RAM or lower the limits on how many concurrent instances of `qmail-smtpd`, `qmail-remote`, and `qmail-local` can be run. While lowering the concurrency limits prevents the system from exploiting concurrency, imposing limits prevents the system from using swap space, and so can increase the system's throughput. On the other hand, if the network bandwidth is saturated, improving qmail's speed is unlikely to improve throughput of messages.

DNS

A commonly overlooked source of bottlenecks is within systems that qmail relies upon to perform its duties. Qmail is most dependent on the DNS system for routing every outbound email. The typical method of accessing the DNS system is via a caching DNS resolver. It performs the necessary recursive queries and stores that information to accelerate future queries. In many cases, this cache is shared between several computers to exploit the overlap in their queries as much as possible. For example, most ISPs provide one or two DNS resolvers for all of their customers. However, widely shared caches have a limitation on the amount of data they can cache. The more computers using a resolver, and the more unique queries made to that resolver, the harder it is for the resolver to cache all of that information. DNS resolvers can only cache a finite amount of information at one time.

It is important to note that email typically results in different DNS lookup patterns than web browsing and other general-purpose network activity. For example, in a company, most email is directed primarily to clients and customers, but receiving email and doing spam-filtering uses DNS-based blacklists or other DNS-based information like DomainKeys or SPF policies—mail frequently uses CNAME, SOA, TXT, NS, PTR, MX, and A records, among others. At the same time, web browsing and other general network activities access a wider variety of DNS names—from news agencies to search engines to advertising hosting companies—but usually use a smaller range of DNS record types: CNAME, SOA, NS, and A records. Funneling all of this activity through a single DNS resolver can force the resolver to remove information from its cache unnecessarily because it does not have enough memory to hold it. Consequently, it is often useful to have a separate DNS cache for a busy email server, allowing it to operate without conflicting with non-email DNS activity.

SMTP specifies that email servers must rely on CNAME, MX, and A records to determine where email messages are sent. Unfortunately, a bug in early, widespread versions of the BIND DNS server (all versions earlier than version 4.9.4) made it impossible to request CNAME records specifically on lame DNS servers, which prevented qmail from delivering mail to such domains. To work around this problem, qmail uses ANY queries, which finds the information necessary for mail delivery, but includes a lot of unnecessary data as well. This unnecessary data is cached by the DNS resolver, and subsequently uses more of the resolver's cache than necessary. Storing this useless information makes the resolver less efficient, and pushes useful data out of the resolver's cache. This bug in BIND was fixed in 1996. Jonathan DeBoyne Pollard has written a patch to qmail (`http://homepages.tesco.net/J.deBoynePollard/Softwares/qmail/` `#any-to-cname`) that removes this workaround and improves the efficiency of the DNS resolver. However, any domains still using the old version of BIND cannot be contacted by qmail once this patch is applied.

There is something else to consider regarding qmail's use of DNS. The BIND DNS client library, the default on many systems, uses a lot of memory—it represents a substantial chunk of the memory required for each `qmail-remote` instance. This is improved by linking qmail against a different DNS client library. There are a wide variety of options, but the one commonly used with qmail, after BIND, is the djbdns library (`http://cr.yp.to/djbdns.html`), also written by Dr. Bernstein. A package, written by Nikola Vladov (`http://riemann.fmi.uni-sofia.bg/programs/` `qmail+djbdns.tar.gz`) makes this procedure relatively simple.

Filesystem

A commonly overlooked system that seriously affects qmail's performance is the filesystem. The organization of the filesystem is critical to qmail's performance in two key places: mail storage and queue storage. The effect of the filesystem on general-purpose mail storage depends on the format used to store mail. Briefly, if mail is going to be stored in Maildir format, each message is a separate file. Thus, the filesystem needs to handle directories containing lots of small files efficiently. If mail is stored in a format such as mbox, the filesystem needs to handle random access within large files efficiently.

The most direct effect the filesystem has on qmail's performance is through the queue. Qmail's queue is considered "crash-safe"; if the computer crashes unexpectedly (for example, if the power goes out) no messages are lost. To do that, qmail writes all information about messages in the queue to disk as it is generated, which generates a large amount of disk traffic.

In addition, the queue behaves similarly to a Maildir mailbox—each message is a separate file in the queue. More accurately, each message is represented by several small files. Just as Maildir mail storage performance is improved if the underlying filesystem efficiently handles large volumes of small files, it also improves qmail's queue performance. Unfortunately, many simple filesystems do not handle large numbers of files in a single folder efficiently. On such filesystems, the names and on-disk locations of files in a folder are stored in a long list, which means the average amount of time necessary to find and open an arbitrary file in such a folder increases linearly with the number of other files in that folder. Ordinarily, this is not a problem. When the queue starts to fill up—if it is unable to deliver mail for a certain period of time, or if the system is under attack by a spammer, or if the system is being used for large mailing lists—the time to find and open files in the queue degrades qmail's ability to deliver mail. If the queue cannot handle large number of files, delivery can quickly slow down. To prevent this problem, qmail splits the queue into several sub-directories (by default, 23). Messages are hashed and stored in the sub-directories according to that hash. If the queue frequently gets very large (greater than approximately 10,000 files per sub-directory), it is wise to increase this split. Some filesystems—such as ReiserFS or EXT3 with directory hashing turned on—are optimized for handling large number of files in a single directory, and on such filesystems qmail's performance can be improved by removing the queue hashing.

It is worth noting, however, that changing the queue hashing-factor (or "split") is a complex task. Charles Cazabon has written a script, `queue-repair` (`http://pyropus.ca/software/queue-repair/`) that alters the queue split, among other useful features. The specific split used by qmail is a compile-time option, and thus changing the split requires recompiling qmail and either trashing or rebuilding the queue.

Silly Qmail Syndrome

The "silly qmail" syndrome is a problem that sometimes crops up in heavily loaded qmail systems. The symptom indicating "silly qmail" syndrome is both processed and unprocessed messages accumulating in the queue and mail not being delivered. This is the result of a minor oversight in qmail's design for high-load environments—specifically, the way `qmail-send` manages the queue.

Whenever it is processing mail in the queue, `qmail-send` performs three tasks, in the following order:

1. Process new messages: determine whether they are for remote or local delivery, and move them from the `todo` section of the queue into the rest of the queue for processing by `qmail-lspawn` and `qmail-rspawn`.

2. Schedule deliveries: search for messages to deliver in the local and remote directories, and command either `qmail-lspawn` or `qmail-rspawn` to attempt delivery.

3. Handle errors: find error messages generated by delivery, and schedule bounce messages as necessary.

When `qmail-send` completes these steps, it either waits for new messages or begins processing newly queued messages.

Unfortunately, preprocessing new messages is a complex and relatively expensive task, as the message must be safely written to multiple parts of the queue. When messages are injected into the queue quickly `qmail-send` can lag behind in processing new messages. Because it is still processing newly queued messages, it cannot progress to scheduling deliveries, and none of the processed messages are delivered and the unprocessed messages stack up as well. A variant of this problem occurs as `qmail-send` waits for current delivery attempts to finish. While it waits, the unprocessed messages stack up, such that when `qmail-send` finally does get to them there is a large backlog, which prevents it from scheduling new deliveries. Unlike the rest of the queue, the `todo` folder that holds unprocessed messages is not hashed (i.e. "split"), and is consequently more susceptible to filesystem-related slowdowns as the number of unprocessed messages grows.

The solution to the problem is to split `qmail-send`'s functionality by having new message processing and delivery scheduling operate independently. Claudio Jeker and André Oppermann wrote a patch to do that, called the EXTTODO patch (http://www.nrg4u.com/qmail/ext_todo-20030105.patch). This patch creates a new qmail component called `qmail-todo` to preprocess all new messages injected into the queue. It sets up a communication channel (a pipe) with `qmail-send` to awaken it after new messages are processed. `qmail-send` then only needs to schedule deliveries and handle error messages. Because `qmail-todo` operates independently of delivery scheduling it is less likely to fall behind in processing new messages, even when they come in quickly. However, if the underlying filesystem cannot efficiently handle large numbers of files in a single directory, the EXTTODO patch may not be enough. To use a hashing mechanism in the `todo` folder similar to that used in the rest of the queue, Russ Nelson has written the BIG-TODO patch (http://www.qmail.org/big-todo.103.patch). Since these two patches often go together, a fellow named Feizhou constructed a combined patch (http://home.graffiti.net/feizhou:graffiti.net/big-ext-todo-20030101). This modification has proven successful in even the most heavily loaded qmail servers.

Summary

This chapter has discussed two primary topics: monitoring qmail, primarily via its logs, and improving qmail's mail-handling speed. Unlike previous chapters, this chapter dealt more with maintaining the qmail architecture than extending it. This brings the narrative full-circle. As emphasized throughout this book, qmail is primarily an architecture for delivering mail. This book examined the qmail architecture from many angles, explaining its components, how to expand it, and finally how to maintain it. With this base of knowledge and approach to qmail, you are well on your way to being a highly effective administrator of a powerful mail transfer agent.

Good luck!

Index

qmail-smtpd
  about 30
  authenticating 31
  email, accepting 30
  email, rejecting 30
  log file 117-119
  log file, expanding 119, 120
  RELAYCLIENT 31
qmailanalog
  about 123
  TAI 123
QMAILQUEUE 35
QMQP
  about 90
  mini-qmail 90
QMTP 36
Quick Mail Queueing Protocol. *See* **QMQP**
Quick Mail Transfer Protocol 36

R

RELAYCLIENT
  POP 32
  SMTP 32
  SMTP-AUTH 34, 35
  tcprules 31, 32

S

Secure Sockets Layer. *See* **SSL encryption**
senders, validating
  about 93
  DomainKeys 95
  SPF 94, 95
sendmail 28
silly qmail syndrome 132
SMTP 32
SMTP-AUTH 34
spams
  challenge-based identifying 101
  heavyweight identifying 99
  identifying 97
  lightweight identifying 98
  mistakes 102
  quarantines 101, 102
  senders, validating 93

  stopping 93
  stopping from getting out 103
spams, stopping from getting out
  bounce-back spam 103
  sender restrictions 103
speed, storage formats
  deleting 60
  delivery 60
  marking 59
  reading 59
  searching 60, 61
speed of operation, increasing
  bottlenecks, finding 128
  concurrency 129
  DNS 130, 131
  filesystem 131
  limits, calculating 127, 128
  resource starvation 130
  silly qmail syndrome 132
SPF
  about 94
  concept 94
  disadvantage 94
  graphical representation 94
SSL encryption
  about 107
  for receiving email 109
  for receiving mail 110
  for sending email 110
  frontend 108
  patch 108
  working of 107
  wrapper 108
static routes 51
storage formats
  about 55
  custom database 56
  features 57
  Maildir 56
  mbox 55
  MH folders 55
  on-disk efficiency 61
  PID 56
  process identifiers 56
  reliability 57
  speed 58

About Packt Publishing

Packt, pronounced 'packed', published its first book "*Mastering phpMyAdmin for Effective MySQL Management*" in April 2004 and subsequently continued to specialize in publishing highly focused books on specific technologies and solutions.

Our books and publications share the experiences of your fellow IT professionals in adapting and customizing today's systems, applications, and frameworks. Our solution based books give you the knowledge and power to customize the software and technologies you're using to get the job done. Packt books are more specific and less general than the IT books you have seen in the past. Our unique business model allows us to bring you more focused information, giving you more of what you need to know, and less of what you don't.

Packt is a modern, yet unique publishing company, which focuses on producing quality, cutting-edge books for communities of developers, administrators, and newbies alike. For more information, please visit our website: www.packtpub.com.

Writing for Packt

We welcome all inquiries from people who are interested in authoring. Book proposals should be sent to authors@packtpub.com. If your book idea is still at an early stage and you would like to discuss it first before writing a formal book proposal, contact us; one of our commissioning editors will get in touch with you.

We're not just looking for published authors; if you have strong technical skills but no writing experience, our experienced editors can help you develop a writing career, or simply get some additional reward for your expertise.

Designing and Implementing Linux Firewalls and QoS using netfilter, iproute2, NAT and l7-filter

ISBN: 1-904811-65-5   Paperback: 288 pages

Learn how to secure your system and implement QoS using real-world scenarios for networks of all sizes

1. Implementing Packet filtering, NAT, bandwidth shaping, packet prioritization using netfilter/ iptables, iproute2, Class Based Queuing (CBQ) and Hierarchical Token Bucket (HTB)

2. Designing and implementing 5 real-world firewalls and QoS scenarios ranging from small SOHO offices to a large scale ISP network that spans many cities

3. Building intelligent networks by marking, queuing, and prioritizing different types of traffic

OpenVPN: Building and Integrating Virtual Private Networks

ISBN: 1-904811-85-X   Paperback: 272 pages

Learn how to build secure VPNs using this powerful Open Source application

1. Learn how to install, configure, and create tunnels with OpenVPN on Linux, Windows, and MacOSX

2. Use OpenVPN with DHCP, routers, firewall, and HTTP proxy servers

3. Advanced management of security certificates

Please check **www.PacktPub.com** for information on our titles

www.ingramcontent.com/pod-product-compliance
Lightning Source LLC
Chambersburg PA
CBHW082120070326
40690CB00049B/4005